SAND IN OUR SHOES

Chasing the American Dream

By
Julian M. King

Illustrations
George E. Johnston

Cover Painting
Anne Coe

Edited and Compiled by
Rosemary Summers Shearer

Terra Rosa Books
Gold Canyon, Arizona

SAND IN OUR SHOES
Chasing the American Dream
A Memoir
By Julian M. King

Edited by Rosemary Shearer

For information address Terra Rosa Books,
3650 S. Blackhawk Rd., Gold Canyon, AZ 85218

First Printing January, 2007

Cover Art by Anne E. Coe
Cover photography by Joanne West
Illustrations by George E. Johnston
Cover and book design by 1106 Design
Photographs not otherwise credited are from the personal papers of Julian M. King

Library of Congress Control Number: 2006907305
King, Julian M.
Sand In Our Shoes: Chasing the American Dream History
1st ed. 256 pages

ISBN-13: 978-0-9786797-0-5
ISBN-10: 0-9786797-0-9

10 9 8 7 6 5 4 3 2 1

Publisher's Cataloging-in-Publication
(Provided by Quality Books, Inc.)

King, Julian M., 1907-1972.
Sand in our shoes : chasing the American dream : a memoir/history / by Julian M. King ; edited by Rosemary Shearer. — 1st ed.
p. cm.
ISBN 0-9786797-0-9

1. King, Julian M., 1907-1972. 2. King, Lucille I., 1905-1999. 3. Kings Ranch Resort—Biography. 4. Kings Ranch Resort—History—20th century. 5. Businesspeople —Arizona—Biography. 6. Couple-owned business enterprises—Arizona—Biography. 7. Resorts—Arizona—Superstition Mountiains—History—20th century. 8. Superstition Mountains (Ariz.)—Social life and customs. I. Shearer, Rosemary. II. Title.

F811.K54 2006 979.1'7504'0922
QBI06-600310

Dedicated to
Julian and Lucy, who started it all

LET THE REST OF THE WORLD GO BY

With someone like you,
A pal good and true –
I'd like to leave it all behind
And go and find
Some place that's known
to God alone,
Just a spot to call our own.

We'll find perfect peace,
Where joys never cease
Out there beneath the kindly sky.
We'll build a sweet little nest
Somewhere in the West,
And let the rest of the world go by

Ernest R. Ball
Keirn Brennan

Let The Rest of the World Go By, popular in the 1940's, was Julian and Lucy's favorite song. The fourth line was the original title of his manuscript.

Acclaim for Sand in Our Shoes:

"A must read for every resident of the Superstition foothills who complains about the dearth of imported cheese at our local supermarket. Those of us with refrigerators, air conditioners and hot & cold running water have no idea of the hardships joyfully undertaken by the Kings who settled this gorgeous place we're now lucky enough to call Home. It should be included in every house closing ."

– *Sherri Harris, Gold Canyon, AZ*

"A delightful reading adventure that details the Kings living out their dream to build a guest ranch from the ground up in our beautiful desert when quite literally, desert living wasn't cool. It is the original B&B."

– *Mary Dougherty, Gold Canyon, AZ*

"Julian and Lucy are icons out of 'The Great Generation.' There's a glamour attached to turning ones back on the big bucks of corporate success and turning Marlboro-man-style to the West. Julian creates suspense with his stories and solidly depicted characters. The tales spin.

– *Ruth Johnson, Gold Canyon, Gold Canyon, AZ*

Acknowledgements

Thanks to: Jack Carlson and Elizabeth Stewart for their support, research and advice; Howard Horinek of the Quarter Circle U Ranch for locating Quick Upton's well while chasing a stray bull; Greg Davis and George Johnston at the Superstition Mountain Historical Museum; Nancy Barkley McCullough and her husband Ken who shared memories and photos; Carl Shepherd, Mary Trout, Vern Haverfield, and Howard and Daphene Downs who helped me track down elusive information; Pinal County's Ernie Feliz, Luis Felix and Carol in Sandie Smith's office; archivists at the ASU Library, AZ State Land Department, and US Bureau of Land Management. Special thanks to Mike Cooney, Sherri and Steve Harris, Ruth and Boyd Johnson, Linda and Doug Norton, Jim and Trish Mosier, Mary Dougherty, and Betsy Lockhart who provided me with advice and encouragement as I wrestled the manuscript into a book

I am especially grateful to my husband Larry for his support of my efforts, my daughter Katy and her husband Ted Washburne, a constant source of inspiration and encouragement, Meg and Jon Morris, Steve, Anne, and especially Alex Shearer, who made the final cover selection.

Rosemary Summers Shearer 2006

CONTENTS

PROLOGUE

THE RESORT IDEA WAS BORN OF THE WAR.

On the little radar antenna deck high on the foremast of the *U.S.S. Enterprise* we used to sit and look out over the ocean, dreaming, planning, and hoping. There were comparatively peaceful periods between actions when we cruised serenely in calm, tropical seas. Beyond the carriers' protecting bulwark of battleships, cruisers and destroyers lay the peace and quiet of an endless blue sea and sky.

The *Enterprise* was a living thing — a personality respected throughout the service and feared by the enemy. Many great fighters served on the "Big E," but no individual personality ever outshone that ship. Her majesty was reflected in the officers and men with the heart and loyalty unsurpassed in any fighting unit, and she inspired in them an eagerness to wade into any scrap and fight to the finish.

She was blessed with capable skippers, a seasoned and loyal crew, and first-rate officers. I was proud to serve her as Fighter Director Officer.

On quiet days I would take my mail, some of it weeks old, to my aerie on the foremast and drift into the dream world of the service man — memories of the past, visions of the future. Here a man's thinking could be as simple and uncluttered as the vast, smoothly rolling ocean that seemed to stretch to infinity.

From this little deck the war seemed grotesque. One day, thundering gunfire, our planes roaring from the decks into the sky, the enemy raining death toward our decks in suicide attacks bent on destroying us. Our men, sweating and straining, some bleeding and dying, setting about to destroy the enemy with our mighty ships and planes. Exploding ships, crashing planes, the sky full of tracer fire.

But the next day, looking out on a calm sea basking in a tropical sun, the fight would seem to have been for nothing. We'd not changed the sea, nor had we even left a track. Half a mile astern the blue water swallowed our wake and only the sweat-smeared charts of yesterday's action showed where we'd been.

Even though we'd again strain and thrill at the next fight, it sometimes seemed futile and meaningless. Our real lives were back home with our loved ones. Our thoughts turned to them when the din of battle died.

For me, the future could be spelled in four letters. L U C Y. Where we had been and the things we had done together formed the substance of my memories; where we would go and what we would do when I got home was the theme of our letters.

We both well knew how casually the war might snuff out our plans, although she was unaware of the details. Almost weekly events, however, made the picture very clear to me. One morning an enemy bomb glanced off a bulkhead within reach of my hand, only to tumble harmlessly onto the flight deck, a dud.

Suicidal kamikaze pilots gave their lives to slash our bow and stern plates, twist the propeller shafts and knock out the generators and gyro, in what the official records routinely described as "near misses." Tokyo Rose announced that thirty-two brave kamikazes had dedicated their lives to destruction of the *Enterprise,* and within hours we were under attack by seventeen suicidal sons of Nippon. All but one were shot out of the sky by our planes and guns, but he crashed his bomb-laden plane through our flight deck, blasting the innards of the ship and snuffing out the lives of many shipmates, including two young officers under my direction.

With each event, our dreams, hanging on the slender thread of good fortune, were cherished all the more, and so our letters were filled with post-war plans for an independent life in the country. The resort business popped up more often than any other idea, but we considered many.

A person might raise chickens in some scenic locale with an agreeable climate. Lucy liked chickens when she was a girl on the farm, and had several which were pets. One, "Thumpy," followed her around the yard, perched on her shoulder, and sat in her lap. But whenever Mother served chicken, Lucy lost her appetite, backed away from the table and as soon as possible, went out to the yard to look for "Thumpy."

Chickens leave me cold, so after writing about them for a while, this idea faded.

The literature on chinchillas, cute little South American rodents with regal fur, said they could be raised at home for six cents a month, and, if left alone at proper times, would out-multiply rabbits. In three years, their potential numbers were almost astronomical. It was the fur and how it became coats that didn't appeal to either of us.

We wrote about people who gather lady bugs in the mountains. They swarm at high altitudes during late summer, and all you need is sheets to spread under bushes, and jars to put them in. A vast market of fruit ranchers was poised to buy them to kill harmful pests in orchards.

We read that goat milk brought fifty cents a quart. Bees had their fling in our imaginations, but all these animal ideas carried aspects for which we lacked enthusiasm.

Writing. What a life of independence and ease, to be an author! We could live where we wished, write what we wanted, and toss routine out the window. If we'd had any confidence in our ability to make a living, that notion would have blossomed.

The resort idea finally won out. So it came that our correspondence, traveling half way around the globe, dwelt more and more with resorts, particularly guest ranches. Horses, attractive guests, horses, nice people on the front porch, horses, pack trips, chuck wagon dinners, and spellbinding scenery. And horses. That was the life for us.

Lucy and I are westerners by birth. She was "bred and reared" on a farm in Nebraska. I was born in Colorado, and with my parents, moved to a small farming community in Nebraska when I was a boy.

We met at the University of Nebraska on a blind date. I took a shine to Lucy's roommate and Lucy liked mine, so we switched escorts during the evening. It was not until the following year that we met again. From then on we were a team. Shortly after graduation in 1927 we married and moved to Kansas City to meet the greater opportunities we imagined to be found in the big city.

My job as a clerk for a large oil company was respectable, paying the magnificent sum of $145.00 per month. We found a comfortable apartment near the Plaza, and found many new friends.

Each year we got two weeks of vacation, but at the end of this brief parole I always found myself snapped back to that chair behind a desk as though I'd spent the vacation at the end of a stretched rubber band.

In the spring of 1934, on one of those balmy, moonlit evenings when romantic thoughts are likely to sever the restraining cords of convention, we were walking to a movie. As always, our conversation turned to travel. We wanted desperately to see the world — all of it — but my salary covered little more than essentials. The boss was discouragingly healthy, and the only prospect was for a pension in thirty years if I worked hard and showed little enough initiative to avoid trouble with my superiors.

One block from the theater Lucy made a bridge-burning proposal.

"Let's save all our money for three years, quit that old job, and take off. We'll go to all the places we've talked about, see all the things we've wanted to see, and travel until we're plumb broke. How about it?"

In our short six years of marriage, I had learned to respect these hunches of Lucy's. Even when she suggested accumulating a nest egg in only three years, chucking my job, and sacrificing eight years of seniority, it sounded logical.

I don't remember whether the movie hero ever got his gal, but by the time the movie ended I knew my gal had hold of an idea loaded with enough imagination to breed success. As soon as we were out of the crowd I cinched it.

"Let's sail from San Francisco on my 30th birthday."

She replied, "Sure. It'll be a swell birthday party."

The trip was Lucy's idea, so she assumed the initiative in figuring how to save the money. I can save dollars but not dimes, and since we would be having more of the latter, there was our strength. We organized a "sinking fund," putting away a few dollars each payday, carefully budgeting the remainder. When Lucy found a sale at the grocery, the "sinking fund" provided the capital for squirreling away extra supplies at bargain prices.

The fund was more often sunk than afloat, but every little bit helped.

One Saturday special, in the depths of the Depression, was pork roast at ten cents a pound. She bought a whole loin. As we grew a little tired of pork chops, and pork roasts, and pork stew, she reminded me that it was "for the trip."

When we bought new clothes, they were suitable for travel. When we finally sailed we wanted to see the world, not show it what two well-dressed Americans wore. So we planned to take as few clothes as was decent and trained for three years at disguising old clothes and making one garment serve several purposes.

Movies must be within walking distance — anything up to three miles — and not cost more than a dime. Empty bottles were returned for refund, and we saved tips by never having anything delivered to our apartment.

We did weaken one vacation time and bought a $17.00 Ford, drove it to Colorado for two weeks, and were elated to sell it at an $8.00 profit at the end of the trip. This tiny success gave birth to another. When around-the-world trip time came, we bought a used car and sold it in San Francisco for sufficient profit to pay all travel expenses to the coast.

My birthday, April 2, 1937, found us setting sail from San Francisco aboard the flagship of the Japanese N.Y.K. Lines' "Asama Maru." Total resources were a little over $3,000 of which nearly half was already spent for steamer passage. Our rather loose itinerary said we would travel until mid-October. Neither of us had a foggy idea if this money would last the distance, but we'd never know until we tried. If we went broke, we'd have to find a means to get along from that point on. It was a gamble, but the rewards were the justification. The trip was even more successful than we'd dreamed.

Our expectations were fulfilled during our second and third class wanderings in Hawaii, Japan, Korea, Manchu, China, Hong Kong, the Philippines, where we laid over with Lucy's cousin Ruth and her husband, Captain Duran Summers, stationed at an American hospital. On to the Dutch East Indies, Singapore, Malaya, Ceylon, and Egypt, then crowned with an exciting six weeks in Europe.

Reluctantly we landed in New York in late fall of 1937, completely satisfying the promise to ourselves that we had traveled until we were plumb broke. Our fund had dwindled to loose change, not enough to return to the Midwest, so we decided to face reality and stay in the East.

Our philosophy that good fortune comes if you open all the doors and seek hard enough for it, was confirmed during the next four years.

It wasn't long before I landed a job at several times my Kansas City pay in a bustling association headquartered in

Washington, D.C. Eighteen months later we moved to New York to accept a new opportunity in a steamship conference, of which I became Chairman prior to the outbreak of World War II. When the government conscripted our ships I was invited by my principals to recline with heels on desk for the duration and content myself by making periodic trips to the bank with generous salary checks.

This did not appeal to me, and I wound up at 90 Church Street seeking and gaining a commission in the Navy. The Yanks would win and I'd be home soon.

Four years later when I returned from the war, we returned to New York only to sell our belongings, stored by the Navy for the duration. The old steamship chairmanship awaited me at advanced salary, but the die had been cast in the letters Lucy and I had written during the war.

Nuts to starched shirts, polished desks, sixty-story buildings, glittering night clubs. We're going West! We climbed into the '41 Ford convertible we purchased before the war, drove to Chicago and bought a travel trailer at a trade show. Everything we owned was in the little trailer which turned its face with ours toward the setting sun.

1

Lucy and I Discover the Desert

IT WAS EARLY ON DECEMBER 24, 1945 when we first laid eyes on the Superstition Mountains. We had been on the road for four months from New York to Florida to Texas to California, then back to Arizona in search of the perfect place to build our guest ranch. Spread before us was a vast valley stretching toward the sleepy desert oasis of Phoenix.

We pulled the car off the highway near a grove of palo verde trees and stepped out onto the desert. It was a spring-like morning such as Arizona is capable of bestowing in December, and we stood captivated by the awesome spectacle of the Superstitions, towering above the valley floor.

The peaks, slashed by canyons and gorges, seemed continually to change in shape and color as black cloud shadows roamed their cliffs. Brilliant sunlight played over the crags, brightening the lavenders, grays, browns and rusts of its volcanic shoulders. Lush vegetation washed the lower slopes in a mantel of muted greens.

We got out of the car and roamed in the desert for a while. It seemed to invite us to stay, and as we returned to the car, even the little house trailer, which had tugged at our rear bumper these 4,000 miles, seemed content to end its travels and settle here where there would be no more snow on its roof, no ice under its wheels.

We drove toward the mountain, following a wandering dirt track, and within half a mile came upon a secluded spot beside a broad dry wash, sheltered by several large ironwood trees.

"Lucy, let's camp here tonight. I'd feel more like Christmas Eve here than in town, wouldn't you?"

"Good deal," she said and was out of the car before I was.

We parked the trailer under a tree and while Lucy set up housekeeping I built a rock fireplace. It didn't take long, for we were in a hurry to get afoot on this new and exciting territory.

All day we wandered. Each breath of dry desert air brought gratitude for having forsaken city smoke and haze, hustle and bustle. To the south were mountains which our map told us were nearly a hundred miles away. No tall buildings, no roaring buses, no crowds of people to interrupt our solitude. We opened our hearts to the desert and the desert folded us in.

As the sun settled over Phoenix, 45 miles to the west, the cloud shadows shifted, and an entirely new palette bathed the mountain. The earthen tones turned pink, then red, then vermilion, crimson, maroon, and finally a deep blue-purple. Cliffs that seemed smooth were slowly revealed as jagged fingers and columns of rock, whose outlines vanished against the rest of the mountain until sunlight and shadow gave them definition.

The desert silence was like nothing we had ever experienced. We slept soundly and were awakened early by a band of yelping coyotes that seemed within a stone's throw of our trailer. It was sweet music.

We relished a breakfast cooked at our rock fireplace, then leaving our trailer behind we started wandering by car along the rough road-trails of the desert. There were dozens of trails to choose from: wood hauler's tracks, small roadways to prospectors' glory holes, cattle watering holes, and a few half-improved

roads to ranches tucked away among the broken folds of earth and rock which formed the foothills of the Superstitions.

Our meandering led us to the headquarters of a large cattle spread. Huge rock and timber corrals and an ancient bunkhouse built of rock flanked the end of the roadway. A whitewashed picket fence of saguaro ribs enclosed a tidy yard, meticulously kept with flower beds and stone walkways threading among several large palo verde and mesquite trees. A sprawling white frame and rock ranch house stood beneath their shade.

Sheltered in a string of hills on the south and the Superstitions on the north, the place showed a feeling of timelessness and serenity, a home loved by its occupants. We felt like intruders as we opened the gate to enter the yard.

We were greeted by a capable looking woman, past middle age. Her voice was strong and clear, her eyes direct, inquiring.

By the time we introduced ourselves and felt the firm grasp of her strong hand, I knew she had us sized up. Mrs. Barkley invited us in and as we exchanged greetings, her husband sauntered into the room. He was tall and lanky with skin like sun-parched rawhide. He wore scuffed boots and a faded shirt. A rawhide piggin' string instead of a belt was threaded though the loops of his Levi's. A battered, broad-brimmed hat sat flush with his eyebrows. As he sat down he threw the hat onto the floor, plucked a sack of tobacco from his shirt pocket and rolled a smoke. Here was a cow man of the old school.

"That's interesting, you wanting to run a dude ranch," said Mrs. Barkley, when we explained our mission. "My goodness, Dad and I practically ran a dude ranch of our own when we were younger. All our friends used to come out from town of a weekend. We put up and fed twenty to thirty people at a time. It seemed like they all wanted to live here and ride our horses. It kept Dad and me busy to keep enough beef on hand."

"This was pretty tough country to get along in when you first came, wasn't it, Mr. Barkley?"

"Still is tough country for a cow man, but it's tapered off from what it was early on. In them days if a man run out of water he'd pay two bits a gallon to fill his canteen or wagon-barrel. It was a two-day trip to town by wagon or horseback, but we didn't know no better, and didn't mind so much."

Tex Barkley talked quietly, his conversation interrupted every minute or two to relight his drooping cigarette.

"When Gertie and I first moved out here there was still a lot of Apaches. They never harmed us none, but they used to sneak around at night and steal our horses and now and then a beef. Never stole beef to sell, just for their own wickiups. But they'd keep our horses and they weren't no law around to get 'em back, so we was forced to do it ourselves. Me and Uncle Jim and Fred and whoever else might'a been losin' crowbaits would get together of an evenin' and go steal our own horses back from them Indians.

"But they wouldn't stay stole. Coupl'a nights later the critters'd be gone again and we'd have to make another raid. It got to be a reg'lar affair. Kind of a game." Tex looked at his wife and chuckled.

Gertrude Barkley's face lit with a "those-were-the-days" expression. She turned and spoke to Lucy.

"But you know, Mrs. King, we worked awfully hard in those days. Sometimes I wonder how we kept going. We raised two daughters and a son, and except for the time I couldn't ride on that account, I spent most of my life in the saddle. We ran several thousand head of cattle in the Superstition country in those days, and Dad needed me. By the time the kids were two years old I was carrying them in the saddle with me on roundup, and we'd put up for weeks in line camps when we were gathering. And by the time the kids were five-six years old they were riding and gathering just like old time cowpokes! Why Bill was a better hand at six than most of the riders you can hire today.

"You can still find one of our line shacks in Charlebois Canyon," she continued. She called it Charley Boy. "My daughter Anne and I packed all that corrugated iron, lumber, ice box, stove, bunks and junk back there one summer when my youngest daughter was only two, and I carried her on the fork of my saddle and led a pack horse to boot."

We listened as the Barkleys reminisced a while longer about their decades in the desert. Tales of Indians, treating illness in the wilderness, and drought.

"We love the ranch and the Superstitions. Wouldn't live anywhere else," Mrs. Barkley said.

"Lucy and I are starting to feel the same way about these mountains," I said. "Talking with you folks gives a person determination to get started and work it out one way or another. Do you know of any land for sale in this area?"

"We don't have any for sale," Mrs. Barkley said, "but Pearly Bates homesteaded a place a couple of miles northwest of here. He might be willing to sell."

The Barkleys were hospitable, but we sensed that they had reservations about the possibility of new neighbors. I hoped we could make friends of these old-timers who, by sheer toughness of mind and body, had conquered a new and virulent land to create a great cattle kingdom.

We said our goodbyes and tucked the name Pearly Bates away for safekeeping.

After spending a few more days exploring the desert on foot and by car we found ourselves in a yard beside a small cottage whose porch was surrounded with piles of rock. A battered gold pan leaned against the wall by the door. A desert water jug, covered

with frayed burlap, hung in the shade of the porch roof. Picks, shovels, single jacks, miner's drills, an old windlass crank, and all the rusty trappings of the prospecting trade were strewn about the place.

A man of medium height and build appeared in the door. He was clean and neat — the kind of tidiness which told that an industrious woman took care of him. As he stepped onto the porch he clamped a battered Stetson on his head, the brim well down to his eyebrows, as a man who daily faces a bright sun is accustomed to wearing a hat.

"Upton's my name." He held out a gnarled hand which bore the roughness and scars of working with rocks and heavy tools. "They generally call me 'Quick' around these parts because I've got a quick-silver mine. It's a good one, too. It'd make me and several other fellas rich if I could only get the money to start minin'. Won't you folks alight and visit?"

Lucy and I introduced ourselves and we shook hands all around, Quick doffing his hat courteously to Lucy.

"Better have a cool drink of water," he said, as he led us to a corner of the porch where a gallon glass jug, covered with tattered burlap, hung by a foot-long leather thong. "Hope you don't mind drinkin' out of our jug."

He took down the jug, removed the cork and swished the jug, carefully spilling some water over the lip onto the burlap. "Some folks are a little spooky about drinking this way, but, shucks, there ain't no bugs can live in this desert. Just keep the burlap damp and you've got sweet, cool drinkin' water year around.

Don't make no difference how hot it gets, the water in this here jug's always cool. Here, have a slug."

He swung the jug toward Lucy and she took a slug. She handed it to me and I took a slug. Quick's water was cool and sweet, just as he said. A large Scandinavian woman appeared. Her dress was full of her and she was full of energy, conversation and laughter.

"You folks are just in time," she said, "I've just took a chocklut cake outa the oven," and before we could be politely reluctant she handed each of us a huge portion of delicious warm cake. "What you fellers doin' in the desert?" she asked.

We told them of our idea for a dude ranch. "We haven't much money to start with, but we're willing to work if we can get a toe hold."

"Jeepers, you don't need to go buyin' no land. Find ya a little mineral and stake out a claim. Only costs a buck a year to register a claim." Quick ran his fingers through his hair as he spoke. "All this land around here is State and Federal land and you can't get your hands on it any other way. This here is a mining claim we got, and of course, I got a good mine, but maybe you can find one too."

"Hey, Quick! —" Ma jumped up enthusiastically. "How 'bout that old grump from Massyousets? Ain't he gittn' kinda tired of that old dobey of his?" She pointed toward the rolling hills as she added, "He's about five miles vest of here."

"Jeepers, Ma —" Quick got to his feet. "I think you got something there. Old man Bates. He's kind of hard to get along with, King, but his wife is a fine little lady, and you just might be able to buy him out. It ain't far from here, but if you're going to deal with that old rooster you'd better settle down first. He's still got his first nickel and it's been adrawin' interest sixty-five year now. What you do," he commanded, "is to bring that trailer a'yourn up here and set it in right on that little flat down by the well. There's plenty of firewood, you're welcome to all the water you can pump, and if you're settled down comfortable you can just take as much of the year to horse trading as that old guy wants. It won't cost you a cent. And you'd just as well get used to livin' in the desert. A little sand in your shoes will do you good. That's all they are to it!"

After eating the dust of the Ford from coast to coast, our little trailer seemed to heave a sigh of relief as we settled it down in the shade of Quick's sprawling mesquites.

The little flat beside the well was beautiful, as the Uptons promised. The well, which Quick had blasted out of solid rock, was 26 feet deep. Atop the cover sat a pitcher pump which drew all the water we needed. Little did we know how important that well would be, for in the months to come that water was the life blood which made our desert home possible.

Little nuggets of information were pouring into our hands and Lucy and I were not letting one slip through our fingers.

We spent the next few weeks exploring land purchase possibilities. We discovered, after several trips to the Phoenix land office and weeks of poring over geodetic survey maps, that most of the land in the area was owned by the federal government or the Arizona State Land Department. Acquiring it demanded skills and occupations neither of us cared to acquire. As we weren't interested in prospecting or running cattle in order to qualify for settling on government land, it was clear that our only alternative was to find property already "proved" or settled, and a willing seller.

Years ago there was a law permitting homesteading. The land office books showed that two World War I veterans had claimed a homestead on 160 acres of land near the south slope of the Superstitions, but had failed to fulfill the requirement and dropped the claim. Years later one Pearly Bates, formerly of Boston, re-established the claim and proved it up by building a house and working the land.

It looked like a visit with Pearly Bates was inevitable.

2

Bates and The Woman

THE CRUMBLING ADOBE SQUATTED IN A MESQUITE GROVE at the end of a glorified cow trail. Four small, high windows peered suspiciously from beneath a broad overhang attached to a sloping tin roof. An improvised wooden rain trough ran along the front, ending over a ten-gallon G.I. can, concocted by the occupants to salvage rainwater from the desert's infrequent rains. A lean-to constructed of saguaro ribs dangled precariously from the north side of the house. The lean-to was enclosed on the west by an ocotillo bough fence which had taken root and now presented a living wall in scarlet bloom. The structure's sole purpose appeared to be to protect from the blazing desert sun a fifteen-year-old Dodge sedan faded to a shade of grey that suggested a once hopeful yellow.

Lucy and I stepped from our car and looked for signs that the owner was home. We drank in the sheer beauty of the setting. The Superstition Mountains towered to the north and east, and the land sloped gently to the south in a fine stand of palo verdes and hundreds of stately saguaros, the sentinels of the desert.

Our discovery of the old adobe did not come by accident. We had trod many miles of Sonoran desert over the last several weeks, armed with survey maps and compasses in search of *the* perfect spot. Bates's name continued to surface in our search and seemed as likely as any as a prospect, so our hopes were high as we approached.

We heard the creak of hinges and the slap of a screen door closing as a well-preserved man in his seventies stepped to the ground in a manner that was anything but hospitable. It was with some misgiving that I offered my hand and announced my name. We shook hands in silence. I introduced my wife, Lucy, and he allowed her a curt nod.

Pearly Bates was not the world's handiest man with conversation. His weather worn face held eyes sharp and steady, with the squint which comes from looking long distances in bright light. His gait was firm, his body of enough size to lend authority, and his posture was loaded with the dignity of a New England Yankee. An engineer's cap covered his head. He was clothed in overalls and a sleeveless shirt which displayed his sinewy, well tanned arms and hands. His clothing was neatly repaired in many places. A battered brier pipe pivoted on the corner of his lower jaw, making broad gyrations when he finally spoke.

Mrs. Bates, a slight and delicate woman, appeared in the doorway and hesitantly came forward. A friendly but furtive smile played about her mouth, and in contrast to her husband, I felt she was glad to see us.

Our compliments about their views of the mountains and desert were sincere, and it was clear that the Bates' appreciated the beauty of their surroundings.

We learned that they had lived here for 13 years, but escaped to the mountains during the summer to fish.

"There's good fishing in those lakes up in the White Mountains. The Woman and I have a camping place that don't cost us anything. I'll show you a fish I caught last summer."

His voice was pitched just a little higher than he would have liked, I imagine, but it was clear and positive, and he sounded like an educated man with an unmistakable New England accent.

He vanished into the house and returned with a two-gallon jar in which gaped the head of a large-mouth bass pickled in something or other. Later I learned this was his Exhibit A, and every visitor who stopped by was regaled with this grisly evidence of Mr. B's skill as a fisherman. There was a standard story that went with it which included a description of the fishing hole, the tackle, what he said to The Woman, what The Woman said to him, and how much it weighed.

That was the biggest, finest fish ever caught in Arizona, he stated positively. We visited with fair success for about an hour, in the course of which I broached our mission.

"Do you know where we might find some land in this area?"

"Nope."

"Would you sell your land?"

"Well, I hadn't ever thought about selling it."

"If you should consider selling it, what do you think it might be worth?" My fingers were crossed and I knew Lucy was gritting her teeth.

He named a figure well beyond our means. It was the probing offer of a Yankee trader, I thought. Had we accepted, only a pittance of our resources would have remained.

There was nothing to do but treat his remarks as casually as possible, retire gracefully and come back another day.

We returned to the trailer, put a pot of beans on the open fire in the yard and settled down to an evening session of the strategy committee. The situation demanded our best efforts, for the land Pearly Bates owned definitely was our apple.

"What do you think, Lucy?" My voice begged for the right answer.

"This is it!" She half breathed it. "We've just got to have this place for our ranch."

We let two slow days go by before returning with a new plan.

While the car was still rolling up to the house the front door opened and both Mr. and Mrs. Bates emerged. We were encouraged.

I've always been sure the Bateses knew exactly why we were there and were as anxious as we to get right to the heart of the artichoke, but, the best maneuver seemed to be to precede business with some pleasant conversation.

I asked, "How did you happen to come to Arizona, Mr. Bates?"

"You've heard of the Depression, haven't you?"

"I sure have," I replied. "It was tough. Lucy and I were in Kansas City and were lucky enough to keep a job, but it was tough anyhow."

"Those goddam bankers caused it."

I could see we were getting acquainted.

"They raised prices to the sky then pulled out the rug and bought up everything cheap and made billions. Why you take The Woman and me. We worked hard all our lives and borne eleven children and raised seven. I was engineer for the Boston street railways and had $76,000 in the bank when they pulled the rug. The goddam thieves took every penny of it. I didn't have anything left except my tools and they'd have got them if they had known I had 'em. Best goddam tools in New England. I've got every one of them right in that house.

"I decided we wouldn't have any more truck with those damned thieves. I got the best goddam Dodge panel truck in Massachusetts and loaded my tools and The Woman and we came west. I made a sling in the roof of the cab to hold my gun. I've got the best goddam .250-3000 savage you ever seen with a scope and everything else which I made myself — I'll show 'em to you — and I had this .45 in a holster right by the seat where I could get at it right quick. Those fellas won't take Pearly Bates again, I tell you."

The loss of $76,000 was a searing thrust at his pride. In the days that would follow, his conversation was full of the rancor, scorn, and bitterness bred by his loss. The Depression had been a direct adversary of Pearly Bates, compounded exclusively for him, its sole objective to rob him of the fruits of a lifetime of hard labor and thrift. He was a skilled mechanic, an engineer who had learned the hard way by self-education, experience, and dogged application. To be out-thought, out-maneuvered, out-fought by something as elusive as a Depression against which he found no means to fight — it all seemed monstrous, and the first event in his life with which he could not cope.

His was a bitter, hopeless philosophy he seemed bent on deepening, for he often spoke of death as if it were something he almost invited and considered just around the corner. I could understand how a man of such intense pride could be bitter, but his vengeful attitude toward all humans was a fearsome thing.

One consequence was a sordid cruelty toward Mrs. Bates. A timid, wisp of a person, her manners were as delicate as her physique. She seldom spoke and when she did her voice was weak, but pleasant. She rarely ventured a thought of her own, her only statements were those bearing Pa's approval. The only name Pearly ever used for her, whether she was present or not, was "The Woman." We cringed every time we heard it.

At length I proposed that we buy the east eighty acres of the land and take an option on the west eighty, the option to be exercised only when and if they wished to sell it. I also suggested that he accept our trailer as part payment.

"I wouldn't have one of those goddam trailers for anything in the world. They're dangerous and'll tear a car to pieces. No sir, I'll never get cooped up in one of them."

His statement hog-tied that part of our deal, so we pressed it no further. Otherwise the proposition attracted him. It meant some cash in his pocket and, temporarily at least, mollified Mrs. Bates' fear of not having a roof over her head.

The next day, somewhat to our amazement, because it seemed too good to be true, he accepted our offer. It hardly seemed possible, but Pearly Bates had said "yes."

I asked that we handle the transaction through escrow with a Phoenix firm. Alas, that brought the bankers into the picture, and the suggestion was almost fatal to our plan.

If we heard it once we heard it a dozen times. "I'm the only person who ever owned this land. I've a 'paytent' direct from Washington, D.C. It has my name on it, and the government gave the land to me. I tell you it is right from Washington, D.C."

That's all there was to it, and such little things as liens against the land weren't even to be considered. But we wanted a title examination anyhow.

It required several hours of patient discussion to win our point, but Pearly finally conceded on condition that we pay all of the legal expense. Pearly promised to bring his 'paytent' and meet us in Phoenix the next morning.

Lucy and I were secretly pleased with the progress as we shepherded Mr. and Mrs. Bates through the ornate doors of the bank and into the presence of the trust officer.

We deposited the purchase price in cash, and Bates turned over his precious patent and asked for the cash in return. He was told it would be his when the title examination had been completed. We heard again the speech about the patent being direct from Washington, D.C. and violent exceptions to any arrangement under which he would not get the cash immediately.

"You goddam bankers," his high-pitched voice echoed off the gilded ceiling, "just want to keep my money as long as you can and get the interest on it. That's my money and my interest and I intend to have it."

All eyes in the office turned our way as several of "you goddam bankers" glared. Fortunately, our banker looked more like a rancher than a banker, and he patiently and artfully prevailed on Mr. and Mrs. Bates by assuring them they were not the sort of folks who would misrepresent anything, and that there would be no difficulty about winding the whole thing up successfully in short order. Just a matter of form.

The flattery finally cooled Bates, we all signed the fateful papers and Lucy and I had a ranch. This called for celebration.

Recently I answered the local barber's query as to how we were doing at Kings Ranch with "Just fine. Full up for the season."

"Old Pearly Bates would turn over in his grave if he heard that! Did I ever tell you about his coming in here the day he sold you his land? He was really strutting and said, 'Well, Herb, I just unloaded that desert property of mine. Some damnfool sailor came along with more money than sense, and I hooked him good!'"

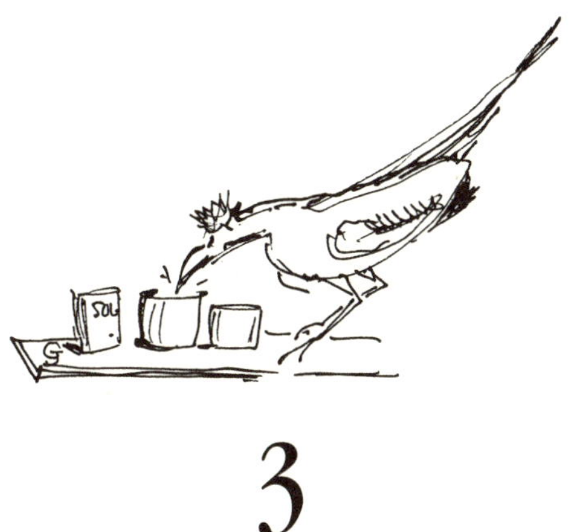

3

Quick Struck it Rich

NOW THAT WE HAD MADE A DEAL WITH BATES, we could start work in earnest.

First we selected a site for our new home. It was on a gentle slope from which we could view all of our new domain. Picacho Peak lay 40 miles to the south, the Catalina Mountains near Tucson eighty miles distant, and countless smaller peaks which seemed to rise out of the broad flat desert as islands rise from the Pacific. To the east lay range after range of mountains with the Pinals in the background. The cragged ridges of Dinosaur Mountain lay close by to the southwest, and the Superstition raised her brooding face in the northerly semi-circle.

Our land. So we called on Bates for his agreement, as nearly a mile of new road must be built to our home site and there was a lot of ground to be cleared. We wanted to start work and move our trailer on the land since the escrow had not been completed. He was willing, even hospitable to the extent of inviting us to park the trailer near their adobe house until we could get our road built.

That being settled, Bates made other conversation.

"During the war the Air Force had bomb targets all over the desert," said Pa. "The targets covered half a section, but they couldn't hit the goddam things with a bomb. They were lucky to get a hit in the same county. Now *I* invented a bombsight that works."

He led us into the lean-to on the north side of the house. It was the shelter for his ancient Dodge, in 1933, an ultra-streamlined model.

"You see this shelter isn't too wide for this car. The first time I drove under it, I had The Woman watch the right front fender to see I didn't hit that post. Goddamned if she didn't tell me 'okay' and turn her back and walk off. When I drove in, the right front fender hit that post, broke it all to hell, and the roof came down on the radiator. Hell, I had to do something, so I made me a bombsight for getting in that garage."

He pointed out a white cloth hung in the center of the far wall and a short white rope dangling from the center of the near edge of the roof. The windshield of his car had a vertical division in the center. On the radiator ornament he attached a spring clothespin with an upright extension which looked like the front sight of a rifle.

"Now when I want to park my car all I do is to line up this windshield divider and that clothespin with the rope and white cloth on the lean-to, and I can't miss. It works perfect. If the goddam army had bombsights like that they might be able to hit their targets. I haven't scratched a fender since I invented this."

We had to admit that anyone with eyes in his head couldn't miss with that invention.

"Now I'll show you something else. Come on over here by the corral." He strutted like a bantam rooster to a small shelter made of ocotillo boughs and old tin signs. The interior was a junk pile of everything the old man had been saving. It was cluttered with ropes, canvas, tin cans, buckets, glass jars, boards, wire netting, flat tires, an ancient cot, and had finally become the home of a nest of pack rats. It was full of cholla cactus balls which the rats brought in to protect themselves from rattlesnakes and Pa.

He pointed to the edge of the roof to which a one by six board was nailed flat. Along the edge of the board six tin cans of varying sizes were fastened. The open ends were pointed to the ground, the closed ends to the sky.

"Now you probably don't imagine what that is. Well, it's my desert pipe organ. My pet roadrunner, 'Jocko' gets up there on that board and beats those cans with his beak and plays music for me."

With a small stone he tapped the tops of the cans to show us the different tones.

"Yes, Sir, by God, he'll play tunes up there by the hour."

We left Pearly Bates to his pet roadrunner and his evening organ recital and returned to the trailer for supper.

That evening we went to Quick's home to tell him and his wife we would be leaving in the morning to take the outfit onto our own-to-be land.

As he heard us coming, Quick swung open the door and said, "King, come here. I've found it! I've found it! And there's hundreds of thousands of tons of the same stuff where this come from."

He picked up two tin cans of rocks, pushed us through the front door ahead of him, and spread the rocks on the table in the light of the kerosene lamp. To me they looked like ordinary rocks, for I didn't then know one from another.

"Look at that, King. See that string of rich stuff in there? God, this is what I've been looking for all my life. I staked out the claim this afternoon."

"You got hunnerts of dem claims," said Ma, her chin hanging low, that same-old-story look in her eye. "Yust about all I heard since ve come here vas, 've struck it rich.' And I still got to do my own vashing and cooking."

"Ma, there's gold in them rocks if I ever seen it. That's all they are to it. It's gold. T'ain't nuthin else, and they's oodles and oodles of it. Ma, it won't be long 'til you've got electric lights, runnin' hot and cold water, a fine automobile and a bathroom with green or pink paper like you always wanted right in your own house. Won't it be wonderful? You won't have to go out back at night. And you can get all the permanents you want."

"I'm believin' it ven I'm seein' it. Sounds yust like the last quicksilver mine you found, but I'm still doin' my business in dat little house out yonder."

A second lady in the room, a stranger until now, spoke up.

"It sure looks like bonanza gold ore to me, Quick. I think you'll get rich on that."

"Nonsense." Ma was a little more than disgusted.

"Oh, excuse me, Daisy, for not introducing you. This is Mr. and Mrs. King who are going to build a big guest ranch near here. They are going to be our neighbors."

Turning to us, Quick continued, "Daisy moved in with us yesterday. She come here suffering from arthritis just like I done twenty years ago, and she'll get just as well as I am now if she stays."

"You ain't much good yerself," chipped in Ma.

"She knows all about ore, King, and she thinks this is good stuff, too. Maybe she'll prospect with me when she gets the hurt out of those joints of hers."

Quick looked younger than when we first met, and was smiling at Daisy like a school boy. Ma didn't share his enthusiasm. She looked like she'd rather have a skunk in the hen coop.

Daisy was doing her demure best to avoid arguments, and depended upon Quick for hospitality. She could have been about twenty-seven, young enough to be pretty, old enough to have that attraction which does not always come with early youth. Her manners and dress were those of a country girl not entirely unfamiliar with the city and its ways, but still — a country girl. She was attractive, especially to Quick.

"Quick," I said, "tomorrow Lucy and I are going to move our trailer on our own land. Pearly Bates says it's okay to park by the adobe house until we get our road built and can move onto the new home site. We'll be close to our work there, and can get more done. We're sure grateful to you and Ma for letting us stay here and for being so nice to us. Your place seems almost like home, and you'll see us often."

Quick and Ma both said they hated to see us leave, and offered us tools, containers to haul water in and any and all of the many useful articles standing around their place just waiting for the next bonanza mine to open.

"And now until you get a well of your own, you just come here for all the water you want. My well's a good one, and that sweet water will help you. You come get all you want."

That was welcome news, for without water, we couldn't even start construction on our road.

4

Just a Crooked Desert Road

EARLY NEXT MORNING WE LED THE TRAILER to a spot Pearly indicated near the old adobe house. We would stay there until our road was built to the future ranch house.

After settling our rubber-tired household, we set out to mark the road and view our new land. Had we realized the hard work, the sore muscles, the calloused palms and sweat in our near future, our enthusiasm might have been dampened, but I doubt it. We were so thrilled at the entire project that these things wouldn't slow us down, ever.

Laying out the road was getting down to cases, and we spent the rest of the day marking the route. There was no way to bring in the three-quarters of a mile of new road without crossing at least one large wash. This crossing was a key point in the route, so we chose the easiest spot, and proceeded in both directions from there.

We tore old newspapers into sheets about a foot square and weighted them down with rocks at intervals of forty or fifty feet to indicate the center of the new road. If we changed our minds, we just moved the rocks.

In later years, visitors often suggested that our road should be straight like city streets, or section lines in Iowa. Such folks have never built a road in the desert with their own hands. When you face an outcropping of rock and must decide whether the road should plow right through, or take a swing to the left where there is soil or it is smooth, chances are you'll take the swing to the left and not tackle the boulders with a pick and shovel. Or when there is a big ironwood or palo verde tree in your path you are likely to go around it "to preserve that beautiful tree." Thus, desert roads become wandering ones. In my opinion, a straight road through the desert seems dull and out of place.

The next morning we went to Mesa and bought our road-building machinery: a pick, a shovel, a rock bar, a rake, a mattock, two pairs of heavy leather gloves and a second-hand utility trailer. That mattock was an interesting one. It had a broad horizontal blade on one side, a vertical blade on the other, and a handle like an axe. It could be used for chopping brush, for cutting down cactus, or as a ground tool. It was the gadget Lucy could use best, even though it was a little heavy. She also seemed to prefer it for, she said, her "golf follow-through" would work on the mattock and it looked like fun, kicking up divots on the desert.

Lucy's willingness to forsake silk dresses, pink teas, bridge parties, New York apartments, and all other glamorous things, for a rake, mattock, pick and shovel, and a road building job in the desert is something I will always be thankful for, but never understand. She didn't hesitate for a moment, and never complained. She worked beside me in the sun all day, in the evening prepared our dinner, and looked forward with me to the next day with all the thrill that comes with creating something of our own. Together we did what I could never have done alone.

When she swung that mattock into some particularly tough piece of brush, or hit a cactus and it snapped back to stab her, I'd hear some of her golf course language. She used special words saved up for slices, divots, hooks, and swishes and they seemed

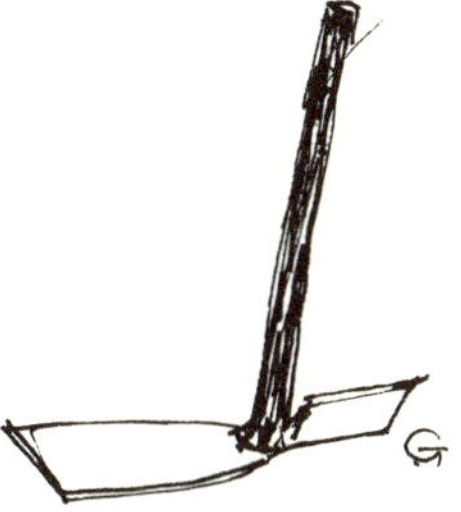

to add extra force to the swing of the deadly mattock. You could almost see the cactus cringe when she addressed it with some of her golf ball curses.

I knew it would be hard work for her, that her muscles would get sore, her palms calloused, but I had not realized how much resolution she possessed. Her acceptance of this hard work and the many privations constantly amazed me. I thought I knew my own girl — I'd been married to her for nearly twenty years — but, I had no idea she had so much stamina. This, combined with her unflagging enthusiasm when the going got tough, egged me into working harder than I ever supposed I could.

After lunch, we walked back to see how much road was completed, and what it looked like. I was amazed that we had covered several hundred yards, and it looked pretty good. We got into the Ford and drove it as far as the road was completed and cherished the thought that ours were the first wheels that had passed this way in all time. There is a great satisfaction in actually creating something.

I looked back to the years which I now considered wasted in an office and wondered what I had ever created. Outside of filling the waste basket daily, nothing ever seemed to have been accomplished.

By the end of the second day we had roughed out our road well enough that we could move the trailer to its new home. The stretch through the big wash didn't look promising. There was a sharp drop to the bottom at the beginning and a steep rise up the other side. The trailer might drag and if we stalled there wasn't much footing for the back wheels of the Ford. We decided to chance it.

At the brink of the wash I put the car in low gear, gunned the motor and we zoomed down and across the bottom. As the Ford started to climb the far bank, the rear bumper of the trailer dug into the soft new road and the whole outfit shivered and hesitated momentarily. The rear wheels of the car threw rocks into the face of the trailer, but we crept slowly forward and soon were out of the wash. No harm done, the trailer soon was parked in a half-acre circular flat among palo verde trees, saguaros, and a good growth of creosote bushes. The view in every direction was magnificent.

We unhitched, leveled the trailer, and settled in. At last, we were living on our own land, and were never happier in our lives.

We cleared and raked the front yard and built a small fireplace of rocks about twenty feet from the trailer door. There was a lot of firewood close by which we gathered and broke into short lengths over a boulder. This method of breaking firewood beat our new axe all hollow, for we were learning that desert wood is brittle and gives to a rock more readily than to a blade.

On February 7, 1946, we carved the date in the bark of the palo verde which shaded our trailer. It was a date to be celebrated annually. A friend in the East had given us a bottle of champagne as a departing token of good luck, and this seemed the time to break it out. Lucy prepared a fine dinner and the champagne provided a fitting toast to our meager beginnings. We turned in at sundown, physically exhausted and sore, but too elated to care.

On the morning of the eighth we went to the adobe in quest of some old boards with which to make a washstand and "biffy." Fragments of sun-baked lumber lay in the Bates' back yard, and I hoped to strike a bargain. I knew that getting what we needed meant money changing hands, but it seemed that future relations would be better if we could make a few reasonable transactions.

The bargaining to acquire enough of those old cracked boards to make a table involved more conversation than would normally seal a good land deal.

I also asked Pearly what materials he had to build a privy. Whatever sanitary arrangement the Bates' used, thus far had been a mystery to us. There was no water in the adobe house, not unusual in the desert, but the customary little outhouse in the rear was nowhere to be seen and we had wondered about it.

"Years ago I started to build a backhouse," he said. "It was a good one, too. It was made of saguaro ribs and was perfect ventilation. I just got it up and was even going to put a roof on when a big wind came along and blew it over. I said to hell with it, and just put the toilet seat on a box and set the box behind a tree. I can move it once a month and don't ever have to dig any holes. So you can have the old outhouse if you want to go around and pick it up. It's still there in the trees where it fell over six years ago."

There it lay, all right, and it certainly was well ventilated. There was no roof, no door, and the spaces between the saguaro ribs varied from a half inch to four inches. We said we'd take it and hauled home this most essential addition to our meager holdings.

Fifty yards downwind from the house-trailer stood a clump of half-a-dozen palo verdes. On the side facing Superstition Mountain was an opening obviously provided by Nature for this purpose.

I dug a hole as deep as the rocks would permit and after redriving the nails which had loosened with their years in the desert sun, we set the new necessary over the hole, with the doorway facing the mountains. The sky served as a roof over the three-foot square opening at the top. By looking through the spaces between the vertical saguaro ribs, one could observe

his surroundings in all directions and be warned of anyone approaching. We outfitted it with a catalog and some old magazines for reading material, and it was ready for serene moments of meditation.

There was no denying it — this was a nifty biffy. We stood off and admired this, the first building on our new land.

With hammer, saw, and nails, I fashioned a wash stand from the boards acquired from Pa. It was a good one, with a shelf for the wash pan and nails for the towels, and we placed it in a clearing twenty feet from the trailer.

The pack rats disputed our possession of the outhouse, for it threatened the domain which had been solely theirs for centuries. They chose weapons nature provided.

The cholla cactus is a tree-like plant usually four to five feet high, the limbs of which bear clusters of cactus balls which resemble strings of link bologna with stickers. It is commonly called "jumping cholla" because each ball is fastened snuggly to its neighbor so that on slightest contact it will detach itself from the chain and impale a hapless intruder with as many stickers as possible. This is a peculiarly devilish experience if the object happens to be your arm or leg. Removing the cactus is a painful and frustrating process, sort of like trying to throw away a loose piece of Scotch tape. You can never shake it loose, and always wish you owned an extra hand, preferably an iron one. Two small rocks, a pocket comb, or the ever-present tweezers came in handy.

Because they detach from the mother plant easily, there are loose cholla balls all over the floor of the desert.

Pack rats know that snakes are in serious trouble if they touch a cholla ball, so the rats fortify their underground homes with great piles of them, cleverly arranged so that any snake attempting invasion is hopelessly snared. A cholla ball barricade is a pack rat's barbed wire entanglement, and is equally effective. No one has ever asked a pack rat how *he* breaks away from one.

That first night the pack rats must have held a conference and decided our new refuge would make a fine mansion for them and their families. They all set out to gather cholla balls, and by morning, a prickly perimeter was drawn across the threshold and around the entrance in a semi-circle twenty feet in radius. They were so ingeniously placed that a human could not walk to the entrance without having his shoes stuck through with barbs.

We raked and burned those obstacles day after day, but the pack rats persisted week after week in building their nightly fortification, even putting pesky cholla balls on the seat and chewing up our catalogs. We never left for a trip to the biffy without a rake and a pair of tweezers.

To crown the glory of our first day's living on the new land, Nature displayed one of those sunsets which only the Arizona desert can afford. The western sky blazed with blue, gold and red, reflected on the cumulus clouds floating in the warm winter sky. The colors were mirrored onto the Superstitions and Pinals to the north and east, painting them with hues no one would believe had they been transferred to canvas.

While the sunset was still glowing I took my daily bath standing plumb naked by the wash stand. It was invigorating to scrub down from a bucket of cold water while viewing that wonderful sunset display. This became a daily ritual for both of us. What a refreshing feeling to be able to bathe in the altogether in the great out of doors, with complete privacy. Nowhere could any other human being or his habitation be seen. If cleanliness was next to Godliness, this certainly was the setting for it.

That night we hooked up our utility trailer, loaded all the cans, buckets and bottles we owned, and set off for Quick's for water.

Where we were raised in the Midwest you could drive a well point a dozen feet, attach a pump, and have all the good water you needed. In the East it seemed that more water was wasted than all of Arizona used. Here, water was dear, and was treated as such.

Quick and Ma greeted us cordially and nothing would do but we should have some cake she just took out of the oven, and take the rest home with us. Lucy's time and facilities for baking were limited, to say the least, so we accepted with joy, for Ma Upton certainly could cook. A pot of coffee was simmering on the wood-burning stove and we joined them in a friendly cup.

Daisy and Quick were smiling at each other but Ma was glum. She said to Lucy, "You better pack up and go to Oregon mit the Vatkins and me. Ve pick fruit up there and make lots of money. Then ve do good fishing ven ve are not picking fruit. Fish *that* long up there." She extended her arms. "Yes sir, you better go. I got some new clothes for going. I vent to town yesterday and bought some shoes, some stockings, and a new gingham dress. And then vat you tink? I bought a hat mit a wail. Look, I show you."

She reached into a corner and brought out her new hat, caressed the veil and set the hat at a jaunty angle, the veil draped over her nose. She swished her hips as she said, "Oh, you better come along. Ve have fun!"

Lucy declined on the grounds that she had rocks to haul, cement to mix and cooking to do. We both wondered, but did not ask, how come Ma was about to take off and leave Quick and Daisy to their own devices while she went fruit picking in Oregon. Something was up.

When we left, Quick went into the yard with his flashlight and returned to the car dragging a surplus barrel which he thought would be helpful for hauling water. We loaded it into the trailer and headed down the hill to the well.

While one of us took a turn at the pitcher pump handle, the other held the bucket to the spout until the bucket was full, then

emptied it into the container on the trailer. Thus we provided ourselves with 70 gallons of water and started cautiously for home. By the time we had completed the nine-mile trip over desert roads, the barrel was only half full, but several days' supply remained. We unloaded and went to bed, dog-tired, but contented.

Tomorrow we would tackle the first steps in our building.

5

"No Beer, No Wife"

WHILE WE WERE LINING UP ALL THE THINGS we would need to lay out the foundation of our house, Lucy began to chuckle. I asked her what was so funny and she said, "I was just remembering the story of the time you fell off the roof."

During my high school days we lived in Central City, Nebraska. My father was doing well in the grain business and when the time came to build a new family house, he offered me a summer job at 35 cents an hour. Good pay in those days for one who knew as little as I. Mr. Rogers, the boss carpenter, was a fine fellow and I guess I did as much work as he expected of the owner's son. At any rate, he was tolerant and we got along.

I had been working about a month. The work on toe-nailing the two-by-four stubs, cantilevered outward along the line of the eaves, which the carpenters called soffits, was nearly done. I was working on the top deck when, like the clumsy kid I was who was growing about six inches a year, I stumbled, fell to the outside, grabbed a long board to halt my fall and, since it was not nailed down, dragged the board down the side of the house, tearing loose at least a dozen outriggers, upsetting the rafter layout, and generally messing up a day's work by the entire crew. Luckily, I was not hurt, but the wreckage was too much. That was my last day on the job.

Such was my only experience in building. I was sure, however, that dumber people than we had built houses and while I probably would do some things unconventionally, I guaranteed our house would stand.

We made stakes out of scraps from the wash stand and took chalk line, level, single jack, pick and shovel to the location of our new home. At the point where the slope was the very nicest we laid out the footings for the 14 by 42-foot ranch house with the front facing a little south of east.

In building a long, narrow house, we again took a page out of the natives' book. It was no accident that most ranch houses were sprawling, rambling things. They were simpler to build and had a distinct advantage in hot weather, for a summer breeze will pass through a house of this shape more readily than through a square structure. Three-quarters of a million folks live in Arizona through the summer so why couldn't we? Besides, we didn't have enough money to do anything else. So, our 10 by 42-foot front porch was designed to catch morning sun in winter, furnish shelter from midday heat in the summer, and make best use of the prevailing southwest breeze.

We fumbled through the process of staking out the floor space and at the end of the first day were satisfied that it was level, square, and of the right dimensions.

Pick and shovel work started the next morning. The point of that pick didn't sink very deep into the rocky ground, underlain as it is with a nasty geological substance called *caliche,* a compacted clay material that frustrates anyone determined to dig a hole. However, every shovelful must be loosened, loaded into the wheel-barrow, and dumped on the downhill side where fill was needed. Lucy helped with the shovel, and we worked together all day under a full head of steam. By supper time a sizeable beginning was visible in the excavation, and we fell into bed early with the satisfaction of having made a good start.

By noon of the next day the digging was well along. Early in the afternoon a car with Connecticut plates rolled to a stop beside our work, bringing our first visitors. We saw the car approaching for nearly two miles and wondered what it was that might be bringing us callers. It was a curiosity, nothing more.

"What in the world are you doing clear up here?"

"We are building a guest ranch."

"A guest ranch!" the lady exclaimed, looking at our small beginnings.

"Yes, this is to be our house, and there will be guest cottages along that slope on the right, and over here to the north. The corrals will be down there just above the wash."

I tried my best to sound like it was all in the bag.

Lucy said, "Don't you think it is beautiful up here?"

"Yes," said the man, "but my God, how will you ever get anyone clear out here?"

We weren't sure, to be frank about it. But it did seem there must be many folks in the world whose love for the beauty, climate and serene silence of the desert would equal ours. Yes, we thought, they would find us just like they found the man with the good mousetrap.

"Our name is King," I said, dropping my shovel and extending my hand. "Where is your home?"

"We are Mr. and Mrs. Prentice from Hartford, Connecticut," the gentleman replied, grasping my hand in his. "We left home about a month ago and are trying to see the West. We like the climate in your country and it certainly is pretty here. Maybe we'll be back as your guests some day." Then on second thought, "I'm not sure my wife would like it this far from town, though."

Mrs. Prentice accepted the challenge. "I guess if other people aren't afraid to live out here in the country, I wouldn't be. And this is a beautiful spot."

"Well, now that you folks have been in Arizona once, you'll come back, and the next time you come, be sure to visit us," I said.

"How about rattlesnakes and coyotes? Aren't you afraid of them?"

"No," Lucy replied, "we hear the coyotes every night and we like them. The snakes are hibernating at this season, and they won't bother us. We don't think they are nearly as dangerous as the drivers on the highway."

"I'd be scared to death," said our visiting lady.

Not until we had some visitors with similar fears did we realize how frightened folks are of the unfamiliar. The larger their home town, and the further east, the greater their fear. We felt then and are surer now that it actually is safer to sleep on the floor of the desert for a year than to venture across a traffic-glutted street in the big city. We will never cease to be amazed at the innocent things which, because they are a new experience, raise morbid fears in the minds of a large segment of the human race.

When Mrs. Prentice learned we had visited Hartford and knew the country well, she warmed considerably. As they left they wished us well, and Lucy and I decided they were our first prospective guests for the following season.

That afternoon another visitor arrived. Across its summit and down the slope of a hill in back of our home site rode a cowboy on a stocky, sorrel horse. As he approached we recognized Tony, a half-Indian, half-Mexican cowboy employed by Tex Barkley, the cattleman who ranched the adjacent range.

Tony's outfit showed signs of hard use. His chaps were frayed at the bottom from riding in brushy, cactus-studded range, the saddle was scratched and worn. Attached to the skirt of the saddle on the left side was a pocket made of an old boot top and rawhide used for holding fence fixing tools. The bridle and reins were of braided rawhide. The man was an artist at making braided horse hair and rawhide articles.

Tony wore a broad smile on his large face. We would learn that he was a friendly soul, always good natured and willing to talk.

"Buenos dias, Meester and Mees King," he said as he dismounted and dropped the reins to the ground. His horse stood, ground-tied. Tony walked over to two sage bushes standing not more than a foot and a half apart, pressed one to the ground and the other on top of the first, then sat on the cushion he thus had made. It was a good trick, and certainly made a softer seat than the rocks afforded.

"What you do, Meester King?"

"We're building a house, Tony."

"Oh-h-h. Thees a good place to build you house, Mees King. I like thees place. Meester Barkley she (Tony never got his hes and shes straight) build house low where me no can see out. I like see out."

"So do we, Tony, and it's why we're building here."

"Oh sure, you see from here feefty, seexty, hunert miles. I like. Over home after I eat nighttime I climb on water tank. You see water tank?"

We could. It stood atop a thirty-foot tower at the base of the small mountain in the distance.

"I sit water tank all evening so I see long way. Every night I sit water tank."

"All alone, Tony?"

"Sure, me all alone. Cowboy always lonesome. Don't see no people. All time lonesome."

"You need a wife, Tony. Why you no catch wife?" You'll find yourself falling into southwestern pidgin-English every once in a while.

"Got no beer. No can catch wife without beer. I catch woman once, but she take off with Mexicano who got beer."

This wife and beer combination was a new one. It deserved further exploration.

"Why not go to town and get a case of beer and then get your wife, Tony?"

"No can do one day. So I go town get case beer. I drink, get borracho, no get wife. When get nuther day off no got beer left. No can get wife."

"Are you sure you can't get a wife without the beer?"

"No, Mees King, I try. I sure."

We had to admit it was really tough.

"How are the folks, Tony?"

"Meester Barkley, she okay. Mees Barkley, he no good right now." It was pretty hard to tell who was okay and who was no good right now. It was a fair guess, however, that Mrs. Barkley was the one who was ailing.

"He gall bladder no work. It jump around. It do this. It do that." Tony illustrated with erratic movements of his hands. "He feel bad and have trouble. Now my gall bladder she no work either. She just lay down and no work. Mees Barkley hes gall bladder she jump all around; mine — she do all the time nothing just like thees." He pointed to his tobacco sack lying on the ground, doing nothing. Gall bladder trouble is not uncommon to cowboys due to their diet of beans, sour dough, and greasy bacon.

The conversation took a half an hour or so. I kept busy all the time with my pick, shovel and wheelbarrow, only pausing now and then to help keep the conversation going. Tony had been watching me carefully. Apparently the amount of hard work going on was disconcerting to him.

"I theenk I ride now," he said as he picked up his Bull Durham and walked toward his horse. "I come back some day when not so much work to do. I tired."

With that he mounted and rode down the hill toward his water tank. Fifty yards from us he turned and waved a final goodbye, the broad grin still on his face.

We went back to work.

6

Cement, Sweat and Tobacco Juice

IT TOOK SEVERAL DAYS TO DIG THE FOOTINGS, haul lumber, and build forms for the concrete foundation. This completed, we leveled the floor area and tamped it firmly.

Our plan was to mix concrete in the wheelbarrow and pour the footings. We were fairly sure we'd need help with the floor. It was a deviation from our plan to build this house all by ourselves, but a necessary one, for we had no mixer and cement must be handled just right.

We turned to Joe Goff, an affable neighbor only fifteen miles away. He and his wife had just built a filling station and new house on their small ranch along the highway. Both the Goffs enjoyed having a bunch of young men around. They weren't related — just young fellows drifting around who had by chance fallen into the good fortune of Goff hospitality. When there was work to do they pitched in and helped. When there was nothing pressing they all had fun. Joe kept a few horses for everyone's amusement, and family rodeos were an almost daily occurrence. He and his wife were jolly, open-handed folks always willing to give a lift or laugh at a neighbor's party.

The boys gathered around as I told Joe we needed help with our floor. Joe said, "Paul, you and Bud don't have anything to do tomorrow. Take the truck and go back in the big wash with King, haul two or three loads of that good sand and gravel up to his place. When you get through we'll load the cement mixer and get Chuck to do the finishing. We'll put that floor down for these folks. I think we can do the whole works for about $45.00, King. How's that?"

"Good deal, Joe," I answered. And it was. It would require two whole days for the crew and involve the use of Joe's mixer, tools, and 120 miles of trucking.

We noticed several small puppies playing about in Joe's yard. They gave me an idea. What is a ranch without a dog?

"Joe, you don't know where a man could get ahold of a dog, do you?"

"My God, yes. Come on. Take four, five, or six — as many as you want. Everyone in the country leaves dogs on our doorstep and one of them dropped a litter of six a few weeks back. Come on out in the yard."

A large black and white mother dog and her six puppies gamboled at Joe's feet. "Take your choice, Lucy. You can have any or all of them."

Five of the pups were spotted black and white. One was all black except for a white blaze running down his chest from the throat. This little pup — "Blackie" was his inevitable name — just sat and eyed us while the other pups scampered about.

"I'd like that little dog, Joe, if it's all right with you," said Lucy.

Joe replied, "Sure you can have him. He's a playful little guy."

Blackie was sitting on the ground in a dream, doing nothing that seemed playful. Joe nudged him hard with his foot and shouted, "PLAY, dammit!"

Blackie ran off with his tail between his legs. At the age of six weeks Blackie had lived about the same span of time as our ranch. He wasn't too sure of himself, but he was a friendly little guy and Lucy was happy with her choice. To Joe's pleas that we take more dogs, we had to turn a deaf ear. One was quite enough at the moment.

The next day Paul, Bud, and I hauled three loads of sand and gravel from the big wash. We really loaded down Joe's old Chevy ton-and-a-half truck, and when we got through, were satisfied we had plenty for the foundation and floor. Joe said the boys would be on deck at 7:00 a.m. the next morning, tools and all.

We had been adding to our water hauling equipment and now owned three oak barrels, a five and a ten gallon cream can, and an old automobile gasoline tank. Nominally we could carry about two hundred gallons of water. As a practical matter it was a lucky day when forty percent of the load didn't slop out from under the improvised canvas lids on the barrels. It was a fair evening's job to drive the nine miles to Quick's, fill all those containers from a pitcher pump, and return home over the dirt road. For the great part of the floor pouring, however, we would have to haul furiously to keep up with the demands of the cement mixer.

So when the day's sand and gravel hauling was completed, Lucy and I loaded our barrels, cans and tanks in the trailer and made the trip to Quick's for water. It was almost midnight when our work was finished and we could tumble into bed. Our muscles were still soft, so they did their share of complaining that night. Once in bed, sleep came over us like a leaden blanket, and we were virtually dead until morning.

We were up bright and early and the water trailer was alongside the job when Paul, Bud and Chuck arrived with the truck, mixer and tools.

Paul Marchand was a tall, husky, bowlegged cowboy, quiet and likeable. He originally came from Detroit and during the war had been a motorcycle courier in the Canadian Army, thoroughly enjoying his many hair-raising experiences, but his one desire was for constant cowboying.

Bud was a round-faced, overgrown boy of perhaps 22, stout, affable, the butt of most of the jokes of Joe Goff and the other boys.

Chuck was from Joe's old home state of Indiana where he had been farmer, blacksmith, carpenter, and general handyman. He was in his middle forties but possessed the fire and energy of a boy. His ruddy face was always creased with a smile, and a fair to middling growth of whiskers displayed ample signs of his prodigious tobacco chewing.

Paul was to charge and run the mixer, Bud would wheel the concrete to the forms in the wheelbarrow, Chuck was the expert who would do the rodding and finishing. Lucy and I were the water hauling crew. Everything, including the ground, had to be wet down before we could start, and this took half our load of water. The remainder was stored in a tank the boys had brought for this purpose.

Paul revved up the mixer and everyone set to work.

It was a great thrill to see that first batch of concrete flow into the forms. It would set, and be there forever. We could not help having that warm feeling of accomplishment, of creating, for this was the floor from which our house would rise.

We headed off again with our water cans for Quick's well. When we returned, the old washing machine gas engine on the cement mixer was puffing away in great shape and the boys had filled about half the foundation trenches. Paul was stripped to the waist and covered with cement splatters from the mixer. Dressed in Levi's, broad western hats and cowboy boots, they made a funny looking crew. But there was nothing wrong with the quality of their work.

At 6:30 in the evening, however, it was apparent we would have to finish after dark. Two old fashioned kerosene lanterns did not offer much light, but there was nothing to do but make the best of it. Chuck was working at top speed to keep up with the setting action of the concrete, and Bud helped him between batches. Our water hauling was done, so I pitched in with the men.

Finally it was all poured, and Chuck was concentrating on the finishing. He produced a bucket of dry cement with which he sprinkled the surface before final troweling. If he found a spot too dry to work properly he wet it up with a good squirt of tobacco juice. It seemed to save Chuck a lot of time and was much easier than using water. Besides, water was so scarce and tobacco juice so plentiful. For an hour and a half Chuck and his tobacco juice troweled the final finish on our floor. Lucy was afraid the brown stain might show, but it doesn't, and she is almost sorry, as it would have made such a good conversation piece.

At 9:30 p.m. the job was done and we were ready for supper, so Lucy fixed frijoles and a pot of coffee and we all sat beside our new floor and relaxed with the good food.

About the only conversation was Paul's compliment to Lucy. "Best damn beans I ever ate."

After the boys left for home, we found ourselves still sitting on a rock beside the new floor, admiring it — almost tearfully — by the flickering light of the kerosene lantern. Had a ballet of exotic dancers appeared before us, I think my eyes would have continued to admire that gorgeous slab of concrete. It was our first permanent mark on the broad expanse of this tremendous land.

7
Water Witches

WATER, A PRICELESS TREASURE IN THE DESERT, was a subject which all but monopolized the conversation of Arizonans.

People who had observed our project, with only one exception that I can recall, all doomed it to failure for lack of water. We were not too sure about it ourselves. Most folks drilled a well before they built a house, and we were asked nearly every day why we weren't doing the same. It was almost too good a question.

One reason was that the title and trust company had not yet issued all the papers necessary for us to show complete title. Until they did, we could not risk our money for drilling.

A second reason was that our funds were so limited we dared not risk a large portion on developing water until we knew best how to take the risk. An expensive dry hole would have wrecked our plans completely, because no money would remain for building rental cottages upon which we must depend for our living the coming winter.

We could not impose on Quick's generosity indefinitely for our own use, nor was it feasible to supply a resort, no matter how small, from his pitcher pump. Sooner or later we would have to attempt to drill a well. If we did not meet with success, as a last resort we would use a tank trailer to haul water from a commercial well where they sold the precious fluid to folks like ourselves. This wasn't a likeable solution, but we were determined to stick it out even in that extremity.

So we decided to "let her ride," in the hope we'd get some ideas which would at least reduce the hazard.

The desert grapevine, always busy, was working overtime. It carried the news that a couple of greenhorns were trying to build a guest ranch at the foot of the Superstitions. The desert lawyers, architects and advisors-in-general hadn't had a chance like this in years, so they were drifting in on all sorts of ruses, hoping to offer the fruits of their experience and imagination to the babes-in-the-desert. Mixed with the chaff were grains of wisdom about developing water.

Our plan was about to start working.

Quick, Ma and her friend, Mrs. Watkins, came to see our new concrete floor. They were the only folks who consistently gave us encouragement, predicting that we could obtain water in a shallow well.

Ma introduced Mrs. Watkins with the remark, "She and me is going to Oregon together. Remember, I told you ve go. She knows all the good places to pick fruit up there, and she knows all about the good fishin'. Oh boy, vill ve eat fish and fruit. Yu know ve make five, six dollar a day! It'll be nice and cool up there this summer."

Then, renewing her invitation to Lucy, "You better go along mit us. Ve girls sure have fun together."

Lucy declined again on the grounds of having to haul rocks for the new house, then turned the conversation to the business of finding water.

Quick claimed that he and Ma could "witch" water, and they brought their friend, Mrs. Watkins, along to help because she was particularly good at it.

We had heard a lot about this mysterious process which had enthusiastic followers and enthusiastic scoffers, about equally divided in number. Neither Lucy nor I placed a great deal of faith in this method of finding water, and could see absolutely no logical basis for it. Why would a forked stick be pulled toward the ground if water lay beneath the surface?

At any rate if the witches were right, as they heatedly argued they were, there was much to be gained, and what could we lose?

Quick went to a creosote bush and cut two forked sticks, stripping off the extra twigs. The branches above the fork were about ten or twelve inches in length, the portion below the fork about two feet. Quick and Mrs. Watkins each took one. Ma Upton said she could feel water by just walking over the ground, so did not need a stick, but Quick and Mrs. Watkins held theirs by the branches with the sticks pointing ahead horizontally.

Mrs. Watkins was reticent about this witching business. Because she was a good friend of Quick's, and Quick was a good friend of ours, she had come only as a personal favor to him. The forked stick, she explained, dipped violently in her hands when she passed over a water bearing area. She did not understand why her body should react in this way and reluctantly concluded that she possessed some powers of witchcraft. She seemed to hold some fear of this endowment. Nevertheless, she was willing to help.

We all strolled into an open area just below the trailer. Quick and Mrs. Watkins started walking, independent of each other, in wide circles. We were all silent, Lucy and I quietly observing every move and hoping the sticks would fairly fly out of their hands. Ma Upton, empty handed, was walking thoughtfully, slowly, in another direction.

Presently, Mrs. Watkins stopped, doubled back, then returned over the ground she had originally covered. We quietly moved in her direction. At one point, the forked stick dipped toward the ground decidedly. This occurred over a strip of ground about six feet wide, and was most pronounced in the center of the area.

After crossing this space several times we all gathered to discuss it, and Mrs. Watkins loosened her grip on the stick to show how the bark had twisted off in her hands. We cut her a new one. Lucy and I both tried the witching wand, but nothing happened. Yet when Mrs. Watkins took the new branch in hand it bent just like the old one, and over the same ground.

Quick and Ma tried the area and confirmed Mrs. Watkins's findings. We had crossed an underground stream, she said, and now she traced it to the strongest spot which we marked with a cairn of rocks.

Quick then cut two straight creosote bush branches about the diameter of lead pencils and two and a half feet long. He handed one to Mrs. Watkins who took it to the cairn, bent down on her knees and grasped the small end of the stick with both hands, much as if it were a fishing pole. She held it perfectly still as we all watched in silence. In a few seconds the thing started pulsating up and down. She counted each dip under her breath. It pulsed down and back just 31 times, and then stood still.

"31 feet to water," said Mrs. Watkins, and all nodded wisely.

She repeated the process for verification, and again the branch stopped throbbing after 31 strokes.

Quick used his stick to repeat Mrs. Watkins' motions. His count was 34 feet, just three feet more than hers.

Ma Upton followed the entire operation in silence. She said she could "feel" the water by sitting on the ground over it. She squatted on the earth in several places along the stream which was marked out, and finally settled beside the cairn. She agreed wholeheartedly that this was the right location.

"Mr. King, you'll find water here in less than 35 feet," Quick proclaimed. "That's all they are to it."

Our faces must have shown the elation we felt, even though this witching business seemed implausible. These folks were pretty positive in their beliefs, and we were not ungrateful enough to question them. After all, on what basis could we doubt, except to say that we didn't understand it?

Quick, Ma and Mrs. Watkins joined us in a cup of coffee at the trailer, and Mrs. Watkins seemed relieved that her powers were no longer needed.

We still hesitated about the well, waiting for we knew not what. Was it a coincidence that others would confirm the findings of these folks?

8

"I'm Not in the Body Today!"

WE HAD DECIDED TO BUILD OUR HOUSE of frame and native stone. The masonry would rise to the window level, the remainder of the wall would be built of boards and battens. If there was one material in this desert which was not likely to give out, it was rocks. They ranged from the size of your fist to the size of a house, and lay on the surface most anywhere one might look.

We backed the hauling trailer to the edge of the wash, loaded it with rocks until the tires looked half deflated, drove to the house, and unloaded alongside the foundation. All day we hauled rocks and by late afternoon, we were reminded of leg and back muscles we didn't know we had. Nevertheless, it was fun because we were doing it ourselves. We were building a rock castle to replace what had been only a castle in the air.

All sorts of strange and interesting things appeared as we worked along the banks of the wash. Now and then we'd find a scorpion hiding in the moist soil under a stone. They were slow and sluggish and at first we flattened them with a stomp of the heel. Never did one manage to sting us. In fact, they didn't seem much interested, they just wanted to be let alone, and we learned to let them have their wish.

Here and there we'd discover an outcropping with a vein of white quartz, or an unusual piece of conglomerate would interest us. These contained all sorts of pebbles in a great variety of colors and shapes, looking like something the devil had mixed in a huge caldron and dumped out on the ground, boiling hot.

Occasionally we found caves where coyotes, badgers and rabbits lived. In the coyote caves were the bones of birds, rabbits and other small animals they had killed and eaten. Huge saguaro cacti seemed to grow out of solid rock banks, as did the palo verde trees. Where they had the misfortune of starting their lives on a curved bank of a wash, flash floods had eroded away the dirt and small stones around the roots. These had become gnarled and they stood like grotesque giants on their crooked legs. The marvel to us was that, despite all this abuse, their lack of soil and the miserliness of heaven with its water, these plants were hardy enough to survive and flourish.

Small lizards, pack rats, rabbits, and high-tails, a local name for a rodent that is a close cousin to a chipmunk, darted from behind rocks and bushes. Blackie was our constant companion, and they kept him at the chase hour after hour. When no small animal was in sight he searched the desert floor on the run, his tongue almost dragging the ground, his tail high and ears erect. When he managed to scare up something the pursuit began with a yipping which we could hear a quarter of a mile away. The short sage brush growing in the flats made it impossible for him to see but a short distance, so he would now and then leap in the air, trying to relocate the game he had lost.

We found where Indians once lived, perhaps a thousand years ago. Fragments of their pottery, pieces of grinding stones and a few specimens were intact and gathered and put in the car. This started us on the trail of becoming avid rock hounds and relic hunters.

Our wall was to be a foot thick and 112 feet long with allowance for four doors. This was the first time we had ever laid one rock upon another, but again we fell back upon the old argument that we had seen people who didn't look any smarter than we are building rock walls. Obviously, they had built a first one, and so could we. With that logic in mind, we started.

We reasoned that a dry rock would suck the moisture from the mortar before it could set properly in this arid climate. Also, if there was dirt on the rock the mortar would not stick. This was to be a perfect wall, so Lucy undertook the washing job and ultimately scrubbed every single stone that went into 112 feet of wall. In later building we learned that we had been overly fussy but the wall stands as sound as the day it was raised. We like to think it will still be standing generations after we are gone and otherwise forgotten.

We weren't going to make any mistakes, but just in case we did it seemed like a good idea to hide them in the most inconspicuous place, so we chose the back corner as the starting point. It would be the furthest from the front door and on the inside it would be concealed by a bed.

The results of the first day were meager. It would take practice, but we had a good start and it didn't look bad.

I stand more than six feet two, and it is a long way to the floor. By night my knees and long back were sore. Lucy was tired too, but never expressed the slightest complaint. We bathed under the trees again, ate heartily, and were sleeping soundly by

8:00 p.m. Each morning we were eager to get back to work, for now the house walls were rising.

We were resting in our trailer after lunch one day when a beat-up panel truck with California tags appeared on the road, then rattled to a stop beside the trailer. Visitors were few and far between so it was always interesting to make acquaintances.

Two men emerged from the truck and introduced themselves as Harold and Wilfred. It was not easy to tell from their attire whether they were prospectors, laborers, horse doctors or horse thieves.

Harold was squat and thick, a man probably in his fifties. His age was camouflaged by a rank, reddish-brown beard which covered him from his eyes to his shirt top. He wore heavy horn-rimmed glasses, an old hat, and well-worn work clothes. His voice was strong, steady, and positive. It was apparent at once that Harold was the talker of the pair.

Wilfred appeared to be older, and not in good health. His voice was weak and squeaky, and he spoke in a rasping whisper. His head was small and sharp, the pallid skin of his face was stretched tight over the nose and small bones, reminding me of pictures I had seen of the mummified head of Ramses II.

Wilfred wore a broad brimmed straw hat perched level on his head, which looked like it had been bought by a woman. His work clothes were covered by a heavy canvas apron that reached from his armpits to his trouser cuffs. Split from the crotch to the bottom, the apron was held around his legs by snaps like the legs of cowboy's chaps.

"What are you folks doing here?" asked Harold, just like it was his business.

"We are building a guest ranch," replied Lucy. Harold's survey failed to reveal much in the way of a guest ranch, and he was plainly skeptical but interested. "We're building our home up there," she added. "The concrete floor is in and we are working on the rock walls."

"Ever done any rock walls before?"

"No, this is the first."

"I've built lots of them," said Harold. "Let's look at it. Maybe I can give you some pointers."

Harold and I went up the hill to the house and left Lucy in conversation with Wilfred.

Harold looked over our first day's work, and watched carefully as I picked up the tools and started the afternoon's labor. Shortly he was freely offering suggestions.

"Now you always want to remember that mud is cheaper than time. Use plenty of mud. It don't cost much and you can go faster. Keep a bucketful of little stones close by for filling in the center. They're just as hard as cement, and they'll save you a lot. Never pick up a rock but what you put it in the wall. Don't waste your time with a lot of fitting. Just put down some mud and set the rock in it. It'll stick all right and you can go on to the next one."

In general, Harold's advice was good, and I found later that he had helped me speed the building substantially.

While Harold was telling me all about rock walls Wilfred was plying Lucy with a constant stream of one-sided conversation.

"Now you take Harold," Wilfred said. "He is a fine fellow, but he thinks he can do everything. There ain't anything he won't say he's done. Now you take right now. He is up there telling your husband all about how to build a rock wall, and he never laid one rock on another. Now you take me. I ain't much concerned about things like walls. I live a spiritual life. I talk with nature and she talks with me. I transfer my thoughts into the minds of others and can make them think what I want them to think. Most of the time I live outside this body in the spiritual world.

"Right now," he continued, gazing at the mountain, "I'm not living in this body that you see. I'm living outside it — out in space. But I'm able to transfer my thoughts to you through my body."

Lucy thought the body looked uncared for, she told me later, and on studying it closely, she could understand why Wilfred preferred to live outside.

Up on the hill Harold and I had talked ourselves out about rocks, and came to the inevitable subject. Water.

"What you doing about water?" he asked.

I explained that we were hauling it for the present, but hoped some day to have a good well.

"Heavens, I'll show you how to dig a well. I can show you right where and tell you how deep you'll have to go."

As he spoke he was walking toward a creosote bush. He whipped out a knife and trimmed up a good stick in much the same fashion Quick had done a week before. Harold grasped the forked ends and started walking back and forth, working his way down the hill toward the trailer.

As we approached, Wilfred could see what Harold was doing and said to Lucy, "Now you take that Harold. He can witch a well right good with that stick. He's the best I ever seen. Now you take me. I never use a stick. My spirit can see right into the ground and tell you where the water is without nothin'. I can see the water right down under the ground."

Lucy blinked and said "How about taking a look around for us?"

"No, not today," said Wilfred. "I'm not in the body today. I only do it when I'm in the body, and sometimes I don't even do it then. It all depends on how I feel. Today I wouldn't feel right if I was in the body."

These obstacles were too much. Wilfred couldn't possibly be of any help today.

Harold and I wandered down the slope below the trailer. He had caught a vein of water and was following it in a north-south line which passed directly beneath the trailer. I managed to get ahead of him as we approached the wash and casually knocked down our small rock cairn with my foot. I was probably fifty feet ahead of Harold at the time, and under the small rise which I'm sure hid my action. He followed the "stream" down over the bank, past the location of the cairn, and across the wash. When he had gone further away from the house than we would want our well, I asked him to return and find the strongest point.

Harold walked deliberately over the entire area, finally stopped at the location of the old cairn.

"Dig your well here," he said. "You'll have lots of good water. Wait a minute and I'll tell you how deep you'll have to go."

He went to a creosote and cut a straight limb about three feet long, grasped the small end firmly in both hands and knelt over the spot. In half a minute the stick started moving up and down, made 35 motions then stopped.

"35 feet," said Harold.

It seemed utterly incredible to me that Nature would associate depth with the man-made measure of twelve inches. The rest of this witching business was puzzling enough, but neither of us could follow any theory that would explain this depth determination. Consequently, we were amazed that Harold's depth of 35 feet was so close to Mrs. Watkins' 31 and Quick's 34. Harold wasn't told of the earlier location, yet had arrived at exactly the same spot and estimated almost the same depth. Maybe they were right.

And if they were, wasn't it wonderful?

Harold and Wilfred climbed into the dilapidated panel truck, started the motor, and rattled down the road. We didn't get a look into the back end of the truck, so have always been curious about its contents. What was the occupation and livelihood of these two interesting characters? It is an odd thing about the desert. Some folks seem to have the knack of living here without working or doing anything very definitive. They wander around, explore, prospect, visit, hunt rocks, live meagerly and

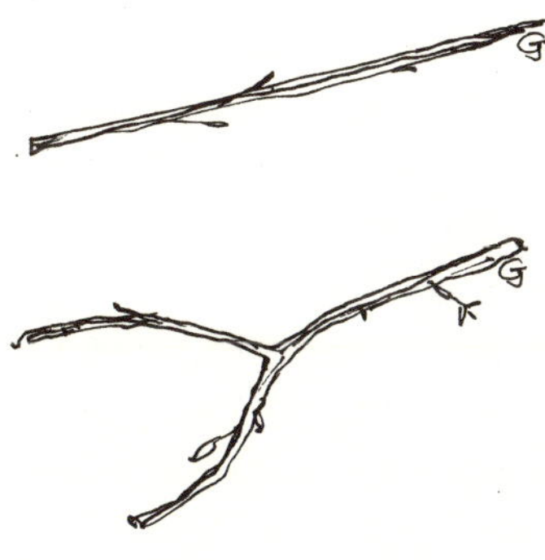

have a wonderful time, apparently on the bounty of the land and climate.

That evening our campfire conversation leaped to well digging like quicksilver leaps to gold. Quick, Ma, Mrs. Watkins, and Harold all led us to the same spot. We concluded we now knew as much as we might ever know about where the water lay, and that it was time we did something about it.

Joe Goff had become our trusted adviser and willing helper in such situations, so we went to his ranch the next evening. We did our talking in the evenings, using daylight hours for building.

We told Joe about our apparent good luck on the water location.

He said, "Well, why don't you go ahead and dig a well? Water is there and it isn't deep. If you want I'll send a couple of the boys up and they'll dig the well for you. A dug well is better than a drilled well anyway."

Joe turned to Bud and Chuck and said, "You boys can put down that hole in a couple of days, can't you?" He said it in about the same way as he had told Blackie to "play" — kind of with a verbal kick in the pants. The boys said they'd do it, at any rate.

"What do think it's worth, Joe?" I asked.

"How's two bucks a foot?"

"Swell. When do we start?"

"Tomorrow morning soon enough?"

It was. Bud and Chuck said they would be up early.

They showed up on schedule with picks, shovels and bars. Before we finished having a cup of coffee together for good luck, Bud said, "I'm not going to start digging in this country until I've had a look around with a forked stick to make sure there's water where we are going to work."

"Can you witch water, Bud?"

"Sure. I've witched good wells here and all over Indiana. My father taught me how, and neither of us has ever missed. But I don't want you to tell me where these other people located. I want to find it by myself. You just show me the general area."

I again dispersed the rock cairn which marked THE SPOT, being careful to see that Bud did not know where it had been. When I gave him the go-ahead, he came out of the trailer and cut a creosote forked stick and started walking in broad circles across the flat. It was not long before his wand responded on the line of the stream located by Quick, Mrs. Watkins, Ma, and Harold. He traced the same water course, but at one point took off on a tangent. Another stream crossed the first one at this point, he said. The newly discovered stream was considerably smaller, or perhaps deeper, than the first. The witching continued and when he came to THE SPOT he said the response was stronger there than anywhere else. Bud was pleased to hear he agreed with the others. I asked about the depth and he got a straight stick and squatted over THE SPOT grasping the small end in both hands. The thing dipped 33 times and stopped.

"33 feet to water," announced Bud.

So the well was started with a pick and shovel at the location of the cairn. We watched for a few minutes, then left the boys to their work and went about our own.

When we went to the well site to invite the boys for lunch, we hoped they might have dug a real pit. I had even thought wishfully about materials for a windlass. Much to our chagrin, they were still on the surface. The hole was not more than two feet deep at the lowest point. Bud and Chuck were sweating and tired, but still determined.

They picked and shoveled that afternoon and all the next morning. By noon of the second day the hole was four feet deep, and everyone was convinced that pick and shovel were no match for the solid rock. Bud and Chuck were not miners with dynamite experience, so we had to call it off.

There was nothing to do but settle back, haul water for a while, until a regular drilling rig could come in and put down the well. Meanwhile other interesting obstacles would claim our attention.

9

Bates Fooled the Bankers

"It's none of their goddam business. If those goddam bankers don't give me my money pretty quick the whole deal is off."

Bates stood next to his car fairly frothing at the mouth, waving papers in the air.

Mrs. Bates sat in the car, trembling. Her lower lip quivered. It was hard to tell whether she was mad at the bankers or afraid of Pearly in his wrath.

"What's the matter?" I asked.

"Those goddam bankers are always prying into someone else's business. They wrote that I'd have to pay the back taxes on this land. It's none of their goddam business. That's between the County and me. Sure, I never paid no taxes. I didn't record the 'patent' so the assessor knew we owned the land. I'm too smart for 'em, by God."

It looked like a smelly kettle of fish. I thought the only way to bring Pearly around was to be firm.

"I had a hunch the bankers would find you'd done something like that and that's the reason I wanted this deal run through escrow," I said. "The taxes are against the land, and if they hadn't discovered that, the County would have been after me to pay for all the past thirteen years. It's a good thing I had them looked into."

"The hell with it! They can all go to hell! And you can go with them. It's no deal!"

Pa's face was red, his pipe was shaking, and the earth beneath him seemed to tremble with his rage.

"The hell with it, nothing," I said. "You signed a deed and the bankers have it, together with my money, your guarantee, and your agreement. You're going to pay the taxes and go through with the deal."

"Oh, I'm too smart for them bankers. Hell, I paid the goddam taxes," he confided, "but the bankers will never find out how much! I fixed *them*. I paid the taxes and gave the goddam bankers the receipted bill, but I took adhesive tape and covered the figures on the tax receipt, and they'll never know the amount I paid. Don't worry, I used to be Chief of Police in Massachusetts, and I know my way around with them fellows."

Well then, he *had* paid the back taxes and given the bank the receipt. Whew! True to his blustery character, his swearing and hell raising were a cover for having given in to the demon bankers, but his show of rage wasn't over.

"I oughta just say to hell with the whole goddam thing. You'll never finish your house. I'm going to stop this whole goddam deal." He thrust the papers into my hand then stomped off across the desert toward his adobe house, leaving his car and The Woman in our yard.

Tears rolled down the little canyons of Mrs. Bates' drawn cheeks. Lucy invited her to sit down and offered her a cup of coffee. As Mrs. Bates' tears subsided, she told us Pearly was really an honorable man who would not break his contract. He wanted to sell the property, she said, because they needed the money. But she was afraid his fits of temper might someday cause a fatal stroke.

She began to tell of her life with Pearly in the desert. As her story unfolded in a shaky, nearly inaudible voice, she gathered confidence and seemed glad to find sympathetic ears into which she could pour the story which had been gnawing at her heart these many lonely years.

She said Pearly had been a hard worker when he was younger, but that when they came to the desert he ceased doing any work unless it was forced upon him. The roof of the adobe house was used as an example.

When they moved in thirteen years ago, the roof leaked like a sieve. During the infrequent rains water poured in at every joint. Pearly immediately recognized the danger of rust to his tools which were piled in the center of the 12 by 24-foot floor. They formed a mound 4 feet wide, 6 feet long and 2 to 4 feet high. It had to be in the middle — no other place would do, Pearly insisted. The one tarpaulin they possessed was used to cover those precious tools. When it rained Ma had to sit on the edge of the bed with an umbrella over her head. When the storm was over, the bedding was dried, pans emptied, and water mopped from the floor.

This situation prevailed for ten years in spite of Ma's protests and the many inconveniences. Finally Pearly was moved to do something about it. The natural thing would have been to re-roof the house, but this was too much work and expense in Pa's view, so he took a shorter course.

The roof was nearly flat with only a slight slope to the front and supported by 2 by 10 rafters which were visible on the inside. Pearly nailed some used slats and roofing paper under the rafters to hold the paper without tearing. The leaking water was captured in the roofing paper, funneled down the slope to the front inside wall into a rain trough made of roofing paper and tin. A rubber garden hose, attached to the lower end of the trough, ran through a hole drilled through the adobe wall into a large can which stood by the front steps. A good rain would provide 15 or 20 gallons of soft water, relieving that problem for days. Not much for aesthetics, but it worked.

Another thorn in Mrs. Bate's side was Pa's refusal to let her clean the board floor because it would raise the grain in the boards. The fact that it literally rained indoors, doing more harm than any scrubbing would ever do, apparently had escaped Pa's skewed logic.

Sweeping the floor would just "stir up dirt and get dust on my tools. You leave it alone, Woman, and don't bother me any more about it," he would shout.

A tidy person who always wanted her house to be clean and presentable, Mrs. Bates was constantly and, often tearfully, embarrassed by the condition of her home. Occasionally when Pearly was gone she stealthily swept the floor, but that was the best she could do. She fairly dreaded the possibility that he might return unexpectedly and catch her in the act.

As she told her story of years of frustration and loneliness, the whole book of their life together opened before her. She talked as though she never wanted to stop. This tale explained things we had observed but not thoroughly understood, such as the lack of an ice box.

There had never been ice in their home, she said, but they had overcome this inconvenience by several resourceful means. A large-surfaced open pan of water always rested on the window sill in warm weather. The passing breeze has enough evaporative action to cool the shallow water for drinking. In another window she placed a vessel with about two inches of water in the bottom with a soup dish inverted so the highest part was just above the water level. Here she placed butter and other perishables, covered by a light cloth, with the ends resting in the water. The cloth acted as a wick. The passing air produced sufficient coolness to keep butter firm in the warmest weather.

From the roof of the lean-to hung two paper bags. Even in the summer heat, she explained, meat could be kept in these. The paper protected the meat from flies and air, and the shade of the roof was adequate protection against the sun. Fresh meat would remain in good condition for more than a week.

In the spring, summer, and fall they moved the sheet iron stove out of doors and cooked in the shade of two large palo verde trees. In the winter the little stove stood in the corner of their one room and provided both heat and cooking.

When Ma and Pearly went to town they put three 10-gallon cream cans in the back of their car. On the way home they filled the cans at a pump for 30 cents per 100 gallons. After they left the highway and started up the desert road Pearly would stop here and there to gather firewood. Combining these chores saved on gasoline and wear and tear on tires and automobile.

"You know, Mr. and Mrs. King, we don't have much money. I don't know what we'd do if it weren't for the $65.00 check we get from the Massachusetts old age pension fund every month. I guess we'd starve, because Pa won't work. Our sons might help, but Pa is mad at them and won't accept a cent. They've come to visit us just once since we've been in the desert, but their stay ended up in a fight and Pa chased them off the place. Generally it's because they took my side trying to get Pa to fix up the house.

"Pa keeps every red cent in his pocket. I haven't had my hands on a single penny, not a single penny, Mrs. King, since we came to Arizona. The boys know that if they send me any money Pa will grab it and I'll never be able to do anything with it, so they stopped sending any. Now and then the girls make me some piece of clothing, but otherwise I never hear from them. My, I love my children, but I don't suppose I'll ever see them again as long as Pa is alive. If he'd die, I guess I'd just wither up and go, too."

Tears welled in her eyes momentarily, but she returned to her story.

She went on to complain about his expensive photographic equipment, which included a quality enlarger, camera and supply of film and the jerry-built darkroom which stood like a shanty inside the front door.

Pearly had shown us his darkroom, bragging about his ingenuity in rigging it.

There was no electricity at the house, but years ago Pearly had swapped something for a gasoline engine off a Maytag washer, and had obtained a small direct-current electric motor which had been converted into a generator driven by the engine. The combination created a small source of electricity, enough for Pa's darkroom but insufficient for lights and other conveniences for which Mrs. Bates yearned.

He refused to buy a clock for timing exposures in the darkroom, but Pa's genius was equal to this need. Two brass tubes from the head of an old bed had been joined and nailed to the inside of the darkroom wall and sloped downward from right to left. At the upper end of the tube a shelf held a dozen ball bearings of various sizes. Under the end of the tube hung an empty three pound lard can. Pearly had demonstrated it to us one day.

"Now these different size balls take different amounts of time to run down the goddam tube. So I took the middle size ball and sloped the tube so the ball would run down and land in the bucket in the time I needed for most exposures. The bigger balls take less time than the smaller ones, so I can get any goddam exposure I want. I borrowed a stopwatch from old man Pruitt and timed the run of each ball. I know which one to use for each exposure. Hell, a man don't need one of those high-priced clock things."

It worked perfectly and never had to be wound.

Mrs. Bates continued her story. "Every time he works in his darkroom he makes me sit still on the bed or leave the house for fear I'll raise dust which might gather on the lens of the enlarger. If I could just scrub the floor it'd be different, but of course I can't do that for fear of raising the grain on those old boards. Sometimes, Mrs. King, I wonder why I don't go crazy."

Lucy made sympathetic sounds.

"And then we don't have a toilet." She blushed as she mentioned this embarrassing fact in my presence. "You don't mind if I talk about it, do you Mr. King?"

I encouraged her to go ahead because I was curious and because she seemed so desperately anxious to unburden herself.

When the wind had toppled the saguaro rib back house Pearly had given us, he simply put a seat on a small box behind a tree. Mrs. Bates said she shuddered every time she used it that a passing cowboy might discover and embarrass her. Each furtive trip, increasingly frequent due to ailing health, was a cause for bitter resentment toward Pa.

"And then, Mr. and Mrs. King… Oh! Here comes Pa. Oh! Never say a word of what I've told you. I don't know what he'd do to me if he knew."

She arose and hastened toward Bates who was digging his heels into the desert floor as he strode straight toward his car in the same rage he had been in when he left.

"What the goddam hell you going to do, Woman?"he yelled over his shoulder. "Stay here all day long? Don't you know it's mealtime? Get in the goddam car, Woman. We're going home."

"Yes, Pearly," said Mrs. Bates as she fluttered up the hill. Neither looked at us again. The engine roared as Bates swung the car around and headed for home, the wheels spitting pebbles in their wake.

Lucy and I stared a little bitterly at the departing cloud of dust. When it had disappeared, she turned and without a word, threw her arms around me and kissed me.

We walked silently to our building site to read the letters Bates had handed me when they arrived.

10

"Look What That Damned Goat Did to Me"

"YOU SHOULD HAFF A GOOD NANNY GOAT," advised Ma Upton that evening when we went for water. "You're working hard and goat milk is real good for you. I got a good Nanny about to kid. I sell her to you cheap. You leave her here until her baby is born, then take her and the kid to your place. She giff good milk and lots of it and someday the kid vill be good to eat. That kid meat suuurre is good. You turn 'em loose and they fertile the whole desert for you."

"I don't know how to milk a goat," countered Lucy, "and I'm not sure Julian would."

"Of course he von't. No he-man vil." Ma was right on the beam. "Come on down to the pen wit me right now, young lady. I show you. I got two nannies need milking."

Ma Upton was big, strong and enthusiastic and literally swept Lucy with her down the path to the goat pen.

As I silently blessed Ma for getting me off that hook, Quick and I settled down to mull over some rock samples from his various claims. He told me about the countless riches waiting in each of his diggings. He claimed his samples contained gold, silver, quicksilver, copper and tungsten. If only someone with money could be persuaded to back him, there was a fortune to be made. His optimism never flagged. It is a way with prospectors. No group of folks on earth has rosier hopes for the future.

"Say, King, she real good at milking goats," said Ma as she and Lucy returned to the porch. "Oh she do yust fine. She's good and strong and knows yust how to squeeze." She demonstrated by squeezing a little air. "That brown nanny vill haff her kid in yust a few days, and then I let you know and you can have them cheap. You sure vill like that milk. It is soooo good for you."

So it was agreed that we would buy the nanny goat.

The next time we went for water Ma came running out of the house with the announcement. "Your nanny had her kid! She sure is cute."

We all trooped to the pen to see them. Sure enough, a tiny white kid was butting his mother's lunch bag. This might be fun. We told Ma we'd pick them up the next day.

"What are you going to name them?" I asked Lucy.

"Ambrosia and Whitey," she responded without hesitation. She must have spent some time choosing that first name. "We'll call the nanny 'Ammy' for short."

That was some improvement. And if I were to escape the chore of milking, I'd better not assert any authority, not even name giving.

The next morning we wrestled woven wire fencing, cut a few posts and built two adjoining pens, one for Ammy and one for Whitey, for if Whitey was with Ammy all the time there would be no milk for us, Ma had told us.

In the afternoon we took the trailer to Quick's and chained Ammy in. Ma had warned that goats devour ropes and straps, so the only way to hold her was with a chain. Whitey rode up front with us, and he was soon in Lucy's lap, sucking her finger, licking her ears and being friendly in every possible way. There was no denying it, he was both cute and smart.

Ammy was chained into her pen and we put Whitey with her for a few days to let him get a start with his mother's milk.

On the third day we separated them. Whitey cried and Ammy tried to butt her way through. She came close enough to success that I had to add boards to the dividing fence. We had alfalfa hay and grain for both, and after feeding Ammy I went into Whitey's pen with a pan of water. As I stooped to place the pan in a corner Whitey ran up my back and stood on top of my head. This became one of the kid's daily tricks and I didn't object unless he tried to chew my hair.

I was never quite sure how Lucy got me to agree to milking when I had time, probably because she generously offered to take over when there was work to be done on the house. I knew I'd have no trouble finding that kind of work to do, so I didn't worry.

One night, however, Lucy handed me a four quart pan and I headed for the pen. I'd milked a few cows but no goats, but Ma had given such a good demonstration that milk started coming after the first few squeezes. Ammy didn't seem bothered as long as there was grain for her. I got about a cup and a half of milk, then it stopped. There was more milk in Ammy's boiler, but she was saving it for her kid. The cup and a half didn't look like much in that four-quart pan.

"She'll give much more in a few days after she's all settled down," I told Lucy, as if I knew all about goats.

The next morning I milked again with the same result. In the evening I managed to convince Lucy that if she would milk Ammy I could put a few more rocks in the wall. She came back with a little more than I had, so it seemed logical for her to continue.

When Whitey was weaned and Ammy had been around long enough to learn where home was we started turning them loose during the day to forage for feed. They ate any and everything all day long and still wanted as much hay and grain in the evening.

Goats want company so Ammy browsed close to where we were working. Occasionally she would come down to the wall, and once she discovered the small chunks of fresh cement on the ground at the foot of the wall, she came several times a day to clean up the scraps. We worried that her milk might turn to mortar, but Ammy's food grinder seemed equal to anything, and she ate cement every day with no apparent damage to her health or milk supply.

The goats, of course, required some of our precious water. We were cooking, bathing, watering two goats and a dog, and mixing two batches of mortar each day with the small supply of water we were able to haul from Quick's. Even though we had learned to economize, our personal consumption was thirteen to fifteen gallons per day. We certainly could have used more milk, but about a pint a day was all we could coax from Ammy. It was precious little for all the trouble of the care and feeding and putting up with the occasional indignities to which she subjected us.

Ammy next discovered that there was nothing like a grapefruit to finish off a good meal of cement. Grapefruit were plentiful and some of our new-found friends in the irrigated flats around Mesa kept us well supplied. We stored them in a sack near the trailer, which Ammy soon found. She found no sport in stealing them when we were out of sight, but she delighted in waiting until we were watching, then she would dart under the trailer, steal a grapefruit and make off into the desert for a nice peaceful feast.

It did no good to shout, throw rocks, or hit her with sticks. She felt no pain and was a showman easily encouraged by the attention her frequent forays attracted.

Undoubtedly the pair wasn't worth the trouble, but she and Whitey furnished entertainment and, as promised by Ma Upton, Whitey would be large enough to eat in a month or so. Neither of us had the heart to do the butchering, but Quick had promised to relieve us of this distasteful chore.

One day I turned Whitey loose with his mother, and the pair went sightseeing. They scampered to the top of a nearby hill, and sampled the feed from all the desert trees and bushes. In the afternoon, they settled in the shade of a tree about fifty yards up the slope from where we were working. They watched us for half an hour then thoughtfully got to their feet and, in a tremendous whirl of speed, ran down the hill to a small patch of castor beans we had planted beside the house, chewed off several tender shoots, then ran back to their cover. In ten minutes they repeated the raid. This time I tossed a rock at them, trying to save the remaining bean plants. They still got one big mouthful before I could prevent it. Fifteen minutes later they were back at it again while I threw more rocks. This was great fun for Whitey and even after Ammy tired of the contest the kid came back time and time again, elated at the attention I gave him by throwing rocks.

But once I accidentally hit him on the front leg. He stopped abruptly, gave me a scorching look, then limped off. Lucy bawled me out for being so cruel and comforted Whitey with as soothing goat language as she could muster. Whitey seemed to catch on. For the next half hour he paced back and forth, back and forth, limping every time the injured foot struck the ground. An outraged look was in his sharp eyes which he affixed on me with scorn. As a final gesture he made off with our milk supply for that day, but I was too ashamed to complain.

About a month later Quick and Ma drove up and asked if we had seen some stray goats. All of theirs had broken out and taken off for the great open spaces. Quick thought the goats

would come to Dinosaur Mountain two miles southwest of our house because when some other goats escaped six years before, they had made their home on the same mountain. Quick's place was over four miles away to the east by beeline.

The large rock knobs on Dinosaur Mountain proved irresistible to the nannies and their kids. There they could take refuge, adjacent to water, safe from man and coyote.

Lucy and I dropped our work, grabbed a sack of grain for bait and headed for the base of the slopes with Quick and Ma. We started climbing. The goats saw us. The oldest was the leader of the flock and kept herself between us and the others. Cautiously we approached the rock knob on which she was standing. Ma took the feed sack in hand and called, "Here, Nanny; here Nanny," in her kindliest manner. The old goat approached within thirty feet and showed signs of taking the bait. If we caught her the whole herd would follow. But she was too smart. When one of us made a false move, she turned and drove the entire herd onto the next higher rock knob.

All afternoon we climbed, called, enticed and used every resource at our command to corner or catch just one goat, but to no avail. Goats can travel where humans cannot.

At length Ma called the chase off with the remark, "I vill come back in my red and white seersucker dress tomorrow. That vill bring 'em on the run. They sure know that dress. It's my feedin' and milkin' dress."

The next day, she returned wearing the red and white seersucker. We went through the entire process again, but the goats all liked their knobby hill and weren't to be moved.

Two days later Quick and Ma returned. Quick had his rifle.

"Those kids are ready for market, and I'm not going to lose all that good meat," he said. "I'm going to shoot the kids down, then the nannies will come home."

Again we all traipsed to the foot of the Dinosaur. Quick loaded his rifle and proved to be an expert shot. Eight rounds brought down the six kids. We took them to the trees along the wash and hung them for skinning.

"I'll take care of Whitey for you while I'm at it." Quick offered.

It was a tough decision. Whitey was cute and a good friend, but obviously would be ninety percent trouble for many months to come. The price of meat was high, and stores were miles distant. The addition to our meager larder would be welcome. Reluctantly we told him to go ahead.

"You go back down by the vash, Quick, and gut them goats," Ma said, "vile I visit mit the Kings. And you do a good yob on that little kid of hers, too."

Quick took orders and disappeared. As soon as he was out of hearing Ma sat down on a broad rock and started to talk.

"I'm pretty yellus of that woman, Daisy. Boy, tings yust ain't right. Yes sir, every time Quick look at Daisy he smile, and every time Daisy look at Quick he smile, and I get more yellus. I don't know vy. That Quick ain't been no good for ten year now. Naw, he ain't no good atall for no woman. You hear him talk you tink he's real good husband, so sometimes I tink I yust let the yoke be on Daisy. Vy should I care? I'm young enough to get me a good man who mean something to me. I'm strong and can vork. Belief me, I can get me a good yob and live vere I don't gotta go out back the house every time I got to do my yob.

"I and Mr. and Mrs. Vatkins goin' to Oregon in a couple of days and ven I come back in a month or so if that Daisy woman still around, belief me the fur vill fly!"

We had to wonder how things would improve with Ma in Oregon for a month, but just nodded in sympathy.

An hour or so later Quick came to the house and handed Lucy a neat package.

"Roast it, Lucy, and add yust a touch of garlic," Ma suggested as she rose to leave. "You sure vill like it and there's eighteen or twenty pounds of good meat there."

Lucy looked at it with dismay, then sighed, and took it into the trailer. Was she thinking of her pet chicken, Thumpy? If so, she never said a word.

Ma was right. It was excellent.

The climax to the goat episode came only a few days later. We had finished breakfast and I was mixing a batch of mortar while Lucy took care of the milking. Ammy had been staked out for several days because we found she could take care of herself on desert feed if she had a chance.

In due time Lucy came dragging back into the house. Her hair hung in tangled strands over her forehead. Her skirt was torn, her arms and face were scratched and, when she came close enough, I could see she was in a crying rage.

"Just look what that damned old goat did to me!"

"What in the world happened?"

"She took off under a palo verde tree and I forgot to let loose!"

It was an awesome picture which arose in my imagination. Ammy charging under a low, thorned tree, through rocks and cactus, with Lucy hanging onto the hind teat like grim death.

I roared with laughter, which did nothing to help the situation.

"You and that damned old goat can both go jump in a cactus patch!"

Tears were rolling down her cheeks and her whole body was shaking with fury wholly in keeping with the ignominy of a ten-dollar goat dragging Her Highness through the cactus.

"Whatcha gonna do, Sweetheart?" I was beginning to feel sorry for Ammy, and would not have been surprised if Lucy had gone for the shotgun.

"I'm going to load that damned old goat in the trailer and take her to town. "

After cleaning herself up, Lucy hunted through boxes until she found some old Christmas ribbon and selected a red bow

which she thought would appeal to a Billy. No show-ring goat ever got a fancier grooming than Ammy, but instinct told her there was an ulterior motive behind it all. She watched with a fishy eye and used every contrary wile she could muster to keep from being loaded into that trailer. Not until Ammy was securely chained did Lucy attempt to tie the red ribbon around Ammy's neck. This was the final insult and the goat nearly stomped through the floorboards in her efforts to get at that ribbon, but my ingenious wife won the round.

Lucy was almost as dirty and disheveled as she was after the dragging, but too mad to change clothes again. She took off with a calculated disregard for rocks and ruts. I prayed the car would hold together until she reached pavement.

It was past noon when Lucy returned. Alone. Humor crinkled her eyes as she waved a tattered red ribbon and a ten-dollar bill at me.

"Here's all that's left of Ammy."

"What happened?"

"She was still so mad when we unloaded her she took after that Billy and nearly wiped up the pen with him. When she thought she had him whipped, she turned disgustingly coy, but he would have nothing to do with her — ignored her with cold scorn. Apparently she had forgotten who was supposed to chase whom in the game of love, and turned on him in another blast of fury. The owner had to let his Billy into another pen to save him. I was so humiliated. I told the man if the Billy didn't want her, I didn't either. The family was short of meat, so he bought her for butchering — O.K.?"

It was more than okay with me, and we spent the ten dollars on the best beef we could buy.

11

It's Great to Be in our Ranch Home

THE WALLS OF OUR HOUSE WERE TAKING FORM. We had built 65 or 70 feet of rock wall and each section looked better than the last. Two of the door frames were installed, giving promise of the structure that was to rise above the rock work. My long back refused to like this kind of work, but I was getting used to the sore muscles.

Lucy seemed tireless. We both labored with as few clothes as the law would allow, and the desert sun had browned us thoroughly. It was a dry winter and not a day had been lost to rain. It now was early April and the whole desert had the look of spring. Here and there wild hyacinths were in bloom. The creosote bushes showed their delicate yellow flowers and the first of the cacti, the hedgehogs, were starting to bloom. Their red and purple flowers were splendid and each day we took just a little time off to admire the new flowers which the spring sunshine was coaxing from their winter sleep.

If we were to sell our trailer, we decided, it should be done soon, otherwise all the winter visitors would be gone and the market would be poor. I ordered a "For Sale" ad run in the

Phoenix papers the following Saturday and Sunday. We told Bates of our plan, and that we would be back on Monday.

"When you sell your trailer, where the hell you going to live? You haven't got a roof on your house."

We admitted we'd just camp until the house was further along.

Our personal belongings were moved into the half-finished home and we took our trailer to market.

Asking price was the same as we had paid. We parked it in an attractive lot in Phoenix, touched it up here and there with paint, made a few minor repairs, waxed the mahogany interior, and made it as inviting as possible. It had been built for a trailer show in Chicago so had some unusual features which should make it easy to sell, and was as comfortable and commodious as its eighteen feet would permit.

On Saturday we had a number of prospects but no buyers. Sunday morning brought more interest, but about 2:00 p.m., Mr. and Mrs. Bates drove up and stepped out of the car. Pearly had a smile on his face! His white shirt gleamed and at his throat was a good looking, black and white tie. His hat was clean and well blocked. His trousers were neatly pressed and instead of the usual tired looking pipe, a king-sized cigar in a rubber holder jutted from his jaw at a cock-sure angle. Mrs. Bates was wearing a fancy wash dress with embroidered frills, newly starched and ironed. On her head sat a perky white hat. The entire outfit was in harmony with the delicacy of her bearing and manner.

"We're glad to see you," I greeted them.

"Just thought we'd come see how you are getting along." Pearly blew great clouds of smoke from his big cigar.

"Well, we haven't sold our trailer yet, but we've got some real good prospects. One party has been here twice."

"That so? The Woman and I been talking about it. Kind of been thinking the trailer might be alright for our fishing trip this summer, if we could make the right kind of a deal. Of course, we haven't got much money, but you talked once about a swap."

"Well now, I suppose we could make a swap." Lucy and I had no idea our luck might be this good. It was hard not to display our elation. "What did you have in mind?"

"How about us taking the trailer in on that other half of the land? The Woman didn't want to sell that half with the dobey house on it because she was afraid I wouldn't put another roof over her head, but she says she'd be satisfied with the trailer. I know where I can get water and park it in the desert next winter for nothin'. It would be handy in the summer up at Springerville. One thing. I'll be goddamned if the bankers are going to have anything to do with this deal! They better get that money to me pretty quick or they'll have a piece of my mind."

I was approaching the same frame of mind about bankers, for it had been close to two months since the matter had been put in their hands. All the long time we waited, we sat on the volcano of Pa's pent up anger at bankers in general and us in particular for bringing him back within their grasp.

The title on the west half was derived from the same piece of paper as the title on the east half, so I could see no reason why we need go through this long escrow business if the bankers cleared the first deal.

"Of course, if we take the trailer I'll have no use for the gas engine and buzz saw and things like that, so I'll sell them to you with the land." Pearly intended to make out as well as he could. "If you'll agree to let us live in the dobey until June 15, you can live in the trailer until May first, then I'll take it over, get it ready for the trip to Springerville and put a trailer hitch on my car. I'll build the best goddam hitch you ever saw. Myself. It'll beat that one of yours all to hell."

In half an hour we had made a deal subject to "those goddam bankers giving me my money" for the first piece of property. It was a fair deal, and at this late date, I couldn't blame him much for making it. But, it was to be an excuse for constant needling for the next month. Almost any reasonable concession would be acceptable to us if it would get us title to all 160 acres and end the eternal bickering. We had never considered ourselves inhospitable, but it would be nice if the fishing season started tomorrow and, some way or another, Pearly could be there for the grand opening.

The trailer was returned to its "home." It seemed to settle contentedly into its old stand, as though this were where it really belonged as a part of our pattern of desert life. We had become accustomed to the old girl, completely enjoying the comfort and hospitality her limited frame offered in our few hours of daily relaxation.

We went to the adobe to pick up our tools, which were part of the new bargain. The main item was the Maytag gas engine. Pearly showed me all the details of its operation, started it several times and had me start it in his presence. Everything seemed to run fine. A bench saw, grinding and buffing wheel, a small electric generator, and an old Packard generator were parts of the outfit. Each unit was mounted so as to slide into the slots on the motor pedestal and be run by the engine. It was an ingenious assembly which we would have much use for in our building. If it worked.

There were also some ground tools, a saw, two planes, a draw-knife and a box of old machine bolts. All were loaded in the trailer.

That engine proved to be the most provoking piece of machinery I ever owned. It was a rope and pulley wheel starter. It would nearly wear out my arms and disposition, and then, when I was almost ready to smash it with a single jack, it would start and run by the hour. Whenever Bates laid his hand on it the engine would start perfectly, and, in his presence, I could start it. But as soon as he left it became as obstinate as ever. Every time Pearly complained about the bankers I complained about the engine. The wrangling over it was maddening to Lucy and several times I thought she was ready to give up the whole thing on that account.

May first, when we were to deliver the trailer to the Bates', was not far away. We decided to concentrate on finishing one half of the house in order to get a roof over our heads by that date.

Compared to the rock work, the carpentry went fast. In no time at all the framing was up and the rafters were clawing at the sky. The wall boards went on easily. The roof sheathing was more difficult because we had to use up considerable crooked lumber which couldn't be wasted.

Lucy and I invented a series of wedges, blocks and pries for influencing uncooperative boards. It didn't take her long to learn how to drive ten-penny nails, and she nailed sheathing boards to the rafters while I pried and wedged.

One day a visiting desert "architect" remarked as he stared at the structure, "Well, she ain't much for looks, but she's hell for stout!"

It was a compliment. We wanted the house to stand forever.

Occasionally we dropped our tools to view the magnificent scene around us. The additional height of the roof opened new vistas. The ever-changing colors on the mountainside, the play of light and shadow on the floor of the desert were amazing to watch. The vastness of this view brought life's mundane events into proper focus and swept away all the discordant and irrelevant details. The few really important things of life and the realities of Nature emerged clearly. They were obvious, unmistakable and logical. Cluttering details were shed like cobwebs swept away by a freshening shower.

How unfettering it was, after years of following the orders of a boss, of constantly scheming to win a promotion or a meager raise, to be doing what we wanted, in precisely our own way, for better or for worse, come Hell or high water.

It was refreshing beyond my fondest hopes to "lay down my hammer" whenever the mood struck me, and admire the gorgeous setting Nature had provided. Lucy's tremendous zest for our new desert life was born of her freedom from social formulae, from the straight-jacket of being conventional. The old life had been "shoveling sand with a fork" — extravagant of energy and substance, with none but artificial, perishable rewards. We both had an evangelistic feeling of glory and new freedom.

We won the race to get a roof over our heads. The walls were incomplete, the windows roughly fitted and unscreened, and doors unhung. Nevertheless we delivered the trailer to Pearly and Ma on schedule and took up residence in the airy semi-shelter of one half-finished room.

Lucy's kitchen consisted of a Number 7 wood-burning stove and a couple of tubs on a bench to serve as a sink. Boxes here and there held the groceries, pans of water with cloths over them cooled the butter and milk. There was a bed, improvised table and two chairs. A kerosene lamp and two lanterns lighted the house in the evenings. Outside the door was the water barrel near the old washstand which had been moved up from the trailer site. It was our bath. A short distance away I constructed an open fireplace for cooking beans and otherwise supplementing the kitchen stove.

At first there was no storage space except the floor. There was no way of providing Lucy immediately with all the household conveniences she deserved, but I set about installing the best kitchen I could. We hung a water barrel on the outside of the house and piped water from it into a kitchen sink. I built some cabinets, shelves and working space, a nice dining table which Lucy decorated colorfully with an oil stain she concocted, and we acquired a few pieces of modest furniture.

We needed a desert cooler, so we built an open frame, with two large shelves about the size and shape of an ordinary icebox. The frame was covered with burlap on all sides. On top we placed a five-gallon putty can donated by the lumberman. Close to the base of the pail I drilled four small holes, one on each side, and put stove bolts through them. When the pail was filled, water dripped through the holes and saturated the burlap covering of the cooler. The flow of water was controlled by tightening

or loosening the four bolts. The box was placed in open shade where any vagrant breeze might cool it. It was amazing how well it worked.

For two hours after sunup and two hours before sunset, however, the box was covered with bees. A swarm had made its home nearby and the water carriers soon discovered this oasis. We found we could open and close the box without getting stung if we moved quietly, so did not particularly mind the attention of our new friends.

In a way, the bees were pets. Their habits were interesting and one could almost set one's watch by their goings and comings.

A small bird bath was built in the front yard from a bucketful of surplus concrete. This attracted birds and rabbits and it was not long until three coveys of quail found the water hole and came regularly mornings and evenings.

The quail were particularly wonderful friends. It was the season when they had their young, and the little ones were so tiny you could hardly see their legs. They seemed almost to float on air.

There was much chatter as the quail family approached, Papa chirping a constant stream of bird talk. Ten or fifteen feet behind him followed Mama with fifteen to thirty young. Papa came to the bath, examined it and the surroundings thoroughly, admonishing his family to stay away until he was satisfied that all was secure. Upon assuring himself he gave the signal to approach. Mama supervised the watering, and let only two of her brood drink at once. When she thought the first two had enough, she chased them aside with her beak and had two more come up. This process continued until all had drunk. Then Papa came and stood guard while Mama drank. Mama guarded while Papa drank, then the Old Man gave the signal and the family departed.

The second and third coveys had stayed fifty to a hundred feet away until the first had finished, then they came up in order.

This was the only open water for more than a mile, and it was not surprising that it encouraged these visitors.

One day in mid-summer I was working alone. Lucy had gone to Mesa for provisions and so far as I knew, there was not a human being within ten miles. Yet I thought I heard women talking. They jabbered like magpies, stopped, then jabbered some more. I lay down my tools and looked around. No cars were in sight, it was too hot for a group of women to venture this far into the desert afoot, yet I could hear their voices.

I took off my hat and scratched my head. "Maybe you've been in the desert too long, King," I said to myself.

Then I discovered a small swarm of flying bugs. I hadn't seen or heard this kind before, but promptly named them "Ladies Aid Bugs." They sounded exactly like the Methodist Church Ladies Aid Society mother had entertained so often when I was a boy.

It was six weeks between our delivery of the trailer to the Bates' and their departure for Springerville. The bankers had completed their work, Bates had our money, and we had clear title to 160 acres of land.

Everyone was happy.

Pearly persuaded a blacksmith in Mesa to let him work at his forge for a day, and there he constructed a trailer hitch for the ancient Dodge. He spent a week more overhauling and retuning the engine.

On the day of departure we went to the adobe house which, in a few hours, would be all ours. The old folks were worn out by the work of moving. The trailer, loaded like a truck, was hitched to the car. The back seat was piled to the roof and on Ma's side in the front other belongings were stacked on the floor.

"That's the best goddam trailer hitch there is," Pearly declared in his loudest voice. "There ain't another one like it in the world. Not the whole world. It ain't no flimsy thing like what you got on your car. Hell, I wouldn't try to go from here to Apache Junction with that rig of yours. Mine'll go anywhere and it'll never break. I made every goddam bit of it, and it's there to stay."

He had always been surprised that the "lousy" hitch on our Ford had lasted the 4,000 mile meandering journey from New York.

"Now you take this car. I've overhauled the whole goddam engine myself. It runs just like a fine watch. Hell, you can't get it overhauled like that in any shop. I done it myself. Hell, I've forgot more than they ever knew. My God, man, I've been in this business ever since automobiles were invented. I know all about 'em."

It must be wonderful, I thought.

At length they pulled away. Privately, both Ma and Pa would have admitted they were scared to death of that trailer, particularly because they must cross high mountain passes en route to Springerville.

Our feelings were mixed as we watched the Bateses leave. Now we would be relieved of all the bickering and bother of mollifying Pa, but we could not help feeling sorry for this unhappy old couple who were uprooting themselves and again changing their mode of living. Heaven only knew what further provocation Pearly might think of to bedevil his patient wife.

We turned to our own problems, glad that at last the land was ours. All ours. Now we could do something real about a well.

All other means having failed, we had screwed up our courage and engaged a professional drilling outfit to come the next day to sink a well where the fateful cairn of rock stood, mutely protecting its secret.

Tomorrow would be a great day!

12

WATER!

"DRILL THE WELL RIGHT HERE."

I pointed to the rock cairn which located the spot the witches promised would lead us to water between 31 and 35 feet beneath the surface.

"How did you pick out that particular spot?" asked George Parsons, who with his son Bert, formed the drilling team of Geo. Parsons and Son, Well Drillers.

"We had some people witch water for us here."

"If you're counting on what water witches told you, you're on the wrong track. This witching is nothing but a hoax. I've fooled those fellows so many times you wouldn't believe it. One day I followed a witch all over a 40-acre field. We used a plowshare to mark the place where he said there was water. I moved the marker half a dozen times without him knowing it, and the stick always pointed down wherever I put the plowshare. There's nothing to it."

That didn't fill us with confidence.

"How *do* you tell where there *is* water, then?"

"You can't in this rock country. Just pick the place where you want your pump and start drilling. If your luck is good you'll get water. You see, it percolates though crevices in the rocks. You get it when you get lucky and hit a crevice."

This was a faith-shattering proposition. Lucy and I had talked day and night about water wells and probably through a process of continuous wishful thinking had made up our minds there was water in the marked spot no deeper than 35 feet. Maybe it was like repeating the same lie until you believe it.

But George and Son gave us not the slightest encouragement about reaching water at a shallow depth. He said he thought we'd have to drill four or five hundred feet in this location. The only consolation we could draw came from their admission that they had never drilled this near Superstition Mountain.

Of course they hadn't. Nobody had ever drilled a well in this vicinity. We were pioneering in that respect, at least. The thought bucked us up a bit.

When the drilling began Lucy and I dropped our work and glued our eyes to the bit. As it sank into the rock with its rhythmic thump, thump, thump, and slap, slap, slap of the cable against sheaves, each of us hoped, hoped, hoped that the witches were right. Drilling had reached 17 feet by noon, when the men stopped to "bail out."

When the thump, thump, thumping approached 30 feet in late afternoon we were tense indeeed. One of the workers stood constantly by the drill, grasping the cable with one hand as though to help the machine. Each time the drill hit bottom the muscles in his arm vibrated with the shock of the flapping cable. He said he could keep a "feel" on the bit in this way.

As the critical depth approached we plied him constantly with questions. Surely, he must be able to "feel" the water coming into the hole. But he always shook his head. Clams are talkative compared to well drillers I have met, and these men would give us neither encouragement nor discouragement.

30 — 31 — 32 — 33 — 34 — 35 feet; the drill thudded on down. To our insistent "No water yet?" there was only a negative shake of the head. 36, 37, 38 feet!

They quit for the day at this point, bailed, and shut down the engine. We all ran our fingers through the muck seeking some sort of clue. The purplish-red mud made with water the drillers had brought and poured into the hole was actually pretty to look at, but it told us nothing. We washed samples in the gold pan on the chance we might find mineral.

No water at 38 feet. It was a tough one to swallow, and a deadly blow to our faith in the witches.

This was Saturday night, a sleepless one. All day Sunday we were prodded by the horns of our dilemma. It would be 36 hours before the drill started again. We could kid ourselves a little about hauling water the rest of our lives but any way we looked at it, that was a daunting prospect.

We decided to take a little trip on Sunday just to change the subject. In the afternoon we stopped to see one of our neighbors. We regarded him as a neighbor even though he was 16 miles from our home. He had lived in the desert for many years, and hauled water from a well five miles distant. His wants were not great, his resources were limited, and he didn't mind too much hauling water. Hundreds of folks in the desert did the same in those days. We had talked to Barney only twice before, but he had seemed such a hospitable, amiable man that we considered him our friend from the first meeting. We told him about our well problem.

"You kids keep right on drilling. What if you can't pay the guy for a while? It won't hurt him and if you are going to have a guest ranch you need water. Maybe they just missed it a couple of feet. You'll get it. You just say 'the hell with it' and keep right on drilling. It'll come out all right. I guarantee it."

How could a person lose faith in his own project when someone else felt as good about it as that? He didn't know, and all of us, including Barney, knew he didn't know. But, sometimes it takes a little damn foolishness to get something done. Lucy and I were bucked up more than we had any right to be.

Just as we were ready to leave, Barney said, "Wait a minute. I want you to try some of the new jam I made the other day. One of my friends sent some fruit and it made delicious jam. Here, take this home with you." He handed Lucy a quart of it. It was a warming thing for a new neighbor to do.

That night we sat on our porch and pondered. We'd never given up on anything yet, and this didn't seem like the time to start. It was one of those incredibly clear summer nights when the stars float lazily in a blue velvet sky above a desert softened, mellowed, by the passing of the day's heat and the descent of the stars' cool glow. It was simply impossible to give up the desert on a night like this.

"Let's shoot the works!"

"Shoot who?" Lucy asked, tumbling out of her trance.

"Let's shoot the works. I've got it all figured out. Tomorrow morning we'll go down first thing and talk to George. I'll tell him to keep right on drilling while I go to town. I'll go to the bank. These bankers aren't much on making desert loans, but I know very well I can talk one of them out of some drilling money. We'll mortgage the ranch if need be. If we ever really get anywhere we've got to finish that well."

Lucy agreed at once. With a definite plan in mind we were able to go to sleep and rest well that Sunday night.

The Parsons had been drilling half an hour or more when we got to the well Monday morning. I asked George to come sit down where we could talk.

I told him we had thought sure he would reach water by now, because all those folks had witched the well. I told him how much money we had, that apparently it wouldn't be enough to go deep like he thought we'd have to. But, I was going to the bank and talk those fellows out of some money. I wanted him to keep right on drilling while I was gone. We were going to shoot the works, and wanted him to stay with us.

It was strictly a monologue. George let me talk, and before I stopped I had told him most of our dreams, hopes and wishes.

When I stopped he said, "Well, I don't think you need tear everything apart quite yet. There was seven feet of water in the hole this morning."

Holy Smoke! The guy had water and hadn't even bothered to tell us or jump up and down and holler or do anything. And 38 minus 7 was 31 feet. Just what Mrs. Watkins had said. I told Lucy and the tears started pouring down her face like she was peeling onions. She threw her arms around my neck and said, "Oh Daddy, I knew all the time we'd hit it."

"How much water do you think we have, George?"

"Not much, but we were able to start drilling without putting any in and we'll probably develop more as we go along. We don't have a well yet, but we may get one. To tell you the truth, I wouldn't have given you a plugged nickel for your chances of getting water this shallow. We'll go on a ways and see what happens. At the end of the day the hole was 17 feet deep with 40 feet of water standing in it.

"Congratulations, King. You've got a well." George announced. "No use of drilling further. I'm going to break down my rig."

It was a pleasure, indeed, to pay George in cash.

That night Lucy and I walked on air, rode the crest of the wave, and rehitched our wagon to a star. What a difference a few buckets of water can make.

A hole in the desert with water in it is wonderful to own, but of no use until you have a pump. Neither of us knew how to install one, be we were determined to learn and to set it ourselves.

We started by pouring a concrete collar and platform around the top of the hole, sealing out insects and surface water.

Two buckets of concrete were left. Lucy said, "We want a shower here by the well for this summer. How about using this extra concrete for the floor?"

So we dumped it on the ground and troweled the mixture into a fairly flat platform three feet square. The shower was never to have wall, curtains, soap rack or any of the ordinary fittings, but it would serve us adequately for many months, particularly through the hot summer.

The Sears Roebuck catalog is a wonderful source for inexperienced folk like us who are distant from the usual sources of information. The "wish book" showed a windmill force pump which would do the trick. We could work it by hand, use a windmill or pump jack and gas engine. The price was only $17.00 so we went to the Phoenix store and bought one, together with rod and all necessary equipment. Our lumber pile contained one piece of 4 by 4 redwood, 20 feet long and a number of 2 by 6 timbers. With these and a log chain we had inherited from Bates, we fashioned a tripod and at the apex attached a single sheave pulley. We ran a rope through the pulley, fastened one end to the rear bumper of the Ford, the other to the well pipe.

We weren't too sure how strong the rope was so I made two pipe clamps out of bolts and 2 by 4 scraps. One would hold the pipe in case the rope broke. It would be a costly matter to have our string of pipe get loose and drop to the bottom of the well.

We screwed the cylinder barrel to the first joint of pipe and attached one end of the rope to it with a screw-eye device I had made. Lucy started the car, eased it forward and lifted the pipe carefully while I guided it. When it was high enough I gave her the signal, she backed the Ford slowly toward the well, lowering our first joint of pipe into the hole. When the clamp came to rest on the concrete platform the pipe stopped, the rope slacked off and we looked the situation over. Our contraption, Rube Goldberg though it was, had worked fine. We were ready for the next section.

As the string of pipe dangling in the well lengthened, of course the weight increased and the added strain on our apparatus began to worry us. I signaled Lucy to raise the pipe so I could remove the clamp. She went ahead, the pipe rose, and I removed the bottom clamp.

Whoooang! Kruuump! The rope parted and the pipe shot into the well with catastrophic drive. Rope ends flew through the air and snapped against the car and tripod. But the safety clamp held. There was the top of the pipe still standing above the surface, the clamp securely in place just below the coupling, the whole contraption quivering. But it held. Our plan was better than the rope!

It was the first of three breaks, but this was the only rope we had and our safety measures were proving adequate, so we went right ahead as though breaking ropes and falling pipes were routine.

Within three hours the entire string of pipe was in the well, and the wooden sucker rod and valves were in place. The pump was threaded onto the last joint of pipe. The entire assembly was lowered onto the bolts that secured the pump to the concrete collar.

"She's done, Honey."

I'm sure my face showed the satisfaction I felt.

"Do you suppose it will work? Will it actually bring us water?"

"I'll show you."

Several strokes of the pump handle brought water to the end of the hose which Lucy was holding. Giggling, she turned the water on me and I kept on pumping until she soaked me properly. Water in the desert. A thrilling sight if ever we saw one. We had whipped our greatest problem and the prospects for our guest ranch were rosier than ever.

That evening, instead of our baths from the bucket beside the palo verde tree, we had the most exhilarating showers of a lifetime. I pumped while Lucy held the hose nozzle over her head and bathed, and she took her turn at the pump handle while I scrubbed. The water was a warm 92 degrees as it came out of the ground. This was an unexpected luxury. It seemed that Nature had gilded the lily just for us.

The next morning we started to town for a gasoline engine and pump jack. On the way we stopped to see our friend Joe Goff, to brag a little about our fine well. Joe, his wife and the boys all seemed pleased by our good luck.

"If you're looking for a pump jack, King, I've got just what you want. It's lying out here in the desert in wonderful shape. I'll let you have it for five bucks."

It was a good buy at the price, so we bought it.

After several cups of coffee and an hour of visiting, the Ford, trailer, Lucy and I headed for Mesa. There we bought a three-horsepower gas engine, shafting, pulleys, belts, bolts — all the things needed to begin our power operation.

When we finally got the machinery all set and started the engine it ran perfectly and water fairly gushed from the hose.

It was real sport to back up the trailer with a couple of empty barrels, start the engine, and sit by while the barrels filled. Our evening showers were even more luxuriant than ever. This pump was our baby and we were justly proud. Lucy kept strict watch of its formula of gasoline, oil and grease, so she could run it if I happened to be busy or away from home.

13

"I Come A-purpose"

WITH OUR NEW WELL IN OPERATION, Lucy could begin landscaping with the desert plants in our front yard. Conventional watering wouldn't work; even the slowest dribbling would run off faster than it soaked in so she used a hoe to make basins on the downhill sides of the plants to hold water near the roots. Usually on Sundays we hauled a couple of barrels of water just for our plants, and were rewarded for the hard work when they prospered in appreciation of our attention.

Building was going as fast as could be expected with only four hands, inexperienced ones, at work. The south half of the house had walls and roof, and was ready for windows and doors. We were snugly settled in the original part, the north half, and each day's improvement added a feeling close to luxury.

Summer had arrived and we wanted to get some guest houses ready for the coming winter season. Money was disappearing at astonishing speed, although neither of us harbored any illusions about it. It seemed impossible to finish our house and build three guest cottages during the remainder of the summer without help, but the bank balance showed it would be impossible to hire a carpenter, pay for material and furnishings, and still have any money left for groceries.

We didn't talk much about the situation, just enough that each of us knew the other was mulling it over. The problem became a beast that wouldn't lie in the corner and keep still. It kept pawing at us, threatening to wreck what we had built.

One evening, as we sat under the bright evening sky, I dragged it into the daylight.

"Lucy, we have to get more money. I'm going to Phoenix to see if I can get a job."

"I'll be sick if we have to stop now," she said. "All our hard work will be lost. If we quit now and move to Phoenix someone might come along and spoil it all for us."

"No," I said, "the way I've got it figured out, I'll get a job at my old profession. We'll still live here and I'll drive back and forth. In the evenings and on weekends we'll do all the work we can, and in time we'll get it done. It'll set us back a year or so, but I can't see any other way."

"The way you love the desert and this work, you'd go crazy in an office, even if you did find a job."

"I kind of agree, but there's nothing to do but try."

So we hauled out the storage barrel in which my city clothes were stored. With her gasoline iron, Lucy pressed a gabardine suit, a tie and white shirt. I found an old brief case and into it went briefs, tariffs, and other samples of my work in New York. Putting on the city clothes was a chore and the damned outfit pulled, choked and bound my body from the cuff of my slick pants to the stiff collar of my shirt. Already I was sweating and wilting Lucy's pressing job.

She kissed me goodbye with the same feeling she had on the dock at San Francisco when I sailed for combat during the war. I felt like I'd rather be going into a free-for-all battle than to a Phoenix office in the clown suit I was wearing. We had little to say beyond "Good luck," and "I'll try to be home before dark."

As I drove I felt as if I were giving up, surrendering to something I ought to be able to whip, and was furious to think I could not be more resourceful. When the forty-mile trip finally ended and I entered the office building where my first prospect maintained his business, my jacket felt like half a dozen blankets around my shoulders, and my spirits were as soggy as my outfit.

My interview was unsuccessful. The gentleman was very nice, but he needed no help and the only other such office in town also was fully staffed.

I was really low and as the elevator descended to the ground floor I jerked off my jacket and tie, opened my shirt at the throat and began breathing again.

"The hell with this idea," I said to myself and headed for home.

Lucy ran up to the car to meet me, her face beaming. "Honey, come up on the porch quick," she almost panted, "there's a lady here who wants to buy some land and build a desert home."

I could hardly believe what I was hearing, but I felt as though I'd just won the Irish Sweepstakes.

Lucy continued, "Her name is Mrs. Wayne. She's an artist from New Jersey. I've shown her a site down beyond the well and she likes it. All you've got to do is name the price and finish the deal. I've got her all sold."

So a miracle occurred. Lucy had done it again, and we were back in business with $500 of good New Jersey cash bolstering our drooping bank account.

We still had a long way to go to get cottages built for winter visitors, but $500 at that point loomed as large as $5,000 would have under different circumstances.

Nails drove easier, boards fit into place with less cutting, and the heat of summer went unnoticed. It was Thursday when Mrs. Wayne bought the land, and by Saturday night we had our house in livable condition so we could start on the cottages.

Sunday should have been a day of rest, but we couldn't stay away from our project. I decided to build a small table on our porch so we might have breakfasts in the shade.

While I was working, Lucy glanced down the road.

"Look at those bowed legs coming up here! It could only be one guy — Paul Marchand!"

The parenthetical walk, broad shoulders, and huge black hat would identify Paul almost anywhere. Something was in the breeze. When you find a cowboy actually going somewhere afoot a thing of importance is driving him. Paul had proved this idea the day we were mixing concrete by telling me of joining a walkout of cowboys at one ranch where he had worked. The boss had ordered the boys to stop riding horses to the back house, and the whole outfit walked out. Including Paul.

"What's the news, Paul?" I asked.

"Well, I'm about to lose my happy home. Joe and his Missus are going to New Mexico to live and there don't seem to be any place for me over there. Besides, I like this country better. I liked your place ever since I first set foot up here, and now I'm kinda hankerin' to join your outfit. I got my own bedroll and fryin' pan so I don't need a helluvamuch to get along."

We had liked Paul's easy-going friendliness, but knowing how a cowboy dislikes any work that doesn't have horses connected with it, I said, "We don't have a horse on the place, Paul, and I don't know when we'll have any. Right now we're busy building and there's a lot of hard work to do. I don't think it's the kind of work you like."

"Well, I don't like any kind of work, s'far as that's concerned. I don't like hard work quite as much as I don't like steady work, but I'm willin' to throw in with you and do my share at whatever there is to do."

"Can you drive a nail straight and cut a board off square?" I asked.

"Well, me and the other boys built Joe's filling station a while back and it's still standin'. It don't look no more cockeyed than any of the rest of them filling stations along Apache Trail." Then he smiled and added, "and someday you'll need some horses and I'll be on the place and can build you a corral and run your horse business for you."

We hadn't had time to decide about horses, but Paul was right that when the time came we'd need a corral and horses.

"Okay," I said. "Bring your bedroll and frying pan and we'll go to work in the morning. If either one of us gets to where he doesn't like the deal we'll just say so and knock it off. Meantime, you're a carpenter, ditch digger, or whatever there is to be done, and Lucy and I'll see that you get along. Sound all right?"

"Sure. My bedroll is behind that palo verde tree right down there. I come a-purpose."

He strode off the front porch and headed for the corral site he already had chosen, picking up his bedroll as he went. He cleared a small space with the toe of his boot, laid out his bedroll, placed his frying pan on a rock, and was all moved in.

Lucy invited him to eat with us until he got a supply of grub. She gave him more utensils and I dug out a small tent which he set up to store his saddle, clothing, old pieces of leather, chaps, prospector's pick and miscellaneous trappings he had accumulated.

Monday morning we all went to Mesa for supplies. Paul and Lucy decided that Paul would cook his own breakfast at his campsite, but would have the other two meals with us. When the trailer was loaded with food and lumber we headed back to the ranch.

We stopped at Joe's to pick up Paul's saddle and war bag, and to tell Joe Goff and his wife goodbye. Joe came out the front door and called, "Hey Lucy, we're going to New Mexico and we've got to get shed of some of these damn cats. You can have the kittens and a couple of more dogs, too, if you want 'em."

"Look, Joe, you got shed of a dog and got shed of a cowboy to us, now you want to give us more dogs and cats. We can't feed any more dogs, but the mice are getting kind of bad, so we might use a cat if you've got a pretty one."

Mrs. Goff came out on the front porch carrying two tiny kittens, a gold one and a dark gray. They were only a few weeks old and looked so helpless nestled against Mrs. Goff's bosom. Lucy's heart melted.

"Gee, Joe, you can't just go off and leave these cute little things on the desert."

"That's what I'm a-tellin' you," beamed Joe, confident of a new home for his problem children. "They're wonderful cats and if you take 'em home you won't have a mouse, rat, tarantula, scorpion, nor nothin' botherin' you from here on out. You take 'em right along, you're sure welcome. Get a sack, Ma," he said over his shoulder, "so the Kings can take these kittens home in the back of their car."

We waved goodbye, a bit sorrowful about having these new and fine friends leave our desert.

As we drove the fifteen miles home from Joe's, we talked about our plans. Paul entered into the conversation as though he had a part-owner's share in the ranch. He already considered himself a member of the family and we sort of liked it.

After unloading the lumber on the site of the new cottages, we took time to play with the kittens and choose names for them.

One kitten was particularly stately and showed prospect of developing into a beautiful cat. He also seemed the most intelligent so I suggested he be named "Brucie" in honor of my father. Father's blood pressure still rises a point or two when either of us call "Here, Brucie," but he is a good sport and finally has become reconciled now that the cat has proved to be both beautiful and intelligent.

"Goldie" would fit either sex and was the obvious choice for the second kitten. He quickly attached himself to Lucy's apron strings and is still her constant pal.

Blackie, to our surprise, accepted the kittens as part of the family, not even protesting when they were fed in his dish, and now all three eat from the same bowl.

One afternoon Lucy was renovating a second-hand icebox in the guest cottage while I was doing some work on the house.

As I raised the protecting sheet of corrugated iron off a low pile of 2 by 4s, I spotted two coiled rattlesnakes, peacefully dozing in the shade. I have never been one to waste ammunition on snakes, but doubting that I could kill both with rocks before one could escape under the lumber pile, and not anxious for an unexpected encounter with the survivor on another day, I went to the house, got my twelve-gauge shotgun, lined them up and killed both snakes with one shot.

I expected Lucy to come running to see what had caused the excitement, but she didn't appear for fully half an hour. When she did saunter down I said, "Didn't you hear the shooting?"

"Sure," she replied without feeling. "What did you do — shoot a snake?"

She was, indeed, getting to be a calloused frontier woman.

14

Superstition Mountain Dew

PAUL, LUCY AND I WORKED TOGETHER WONDERFULLY WELL. The jokes and small talk made the work seem fun. Now and then when "that steady work" started to slow Paul down, Lucy bawled him out as only she could, and Paul would pick up speed again, but usually he had some such remark as, "Tough old squaw, ain't ya?"

We enjoyed this relationship for he never took advantage of our friendship and he was as loyal as a son.

In three weeks the first guest cottage was done. It consisted of only one room and did not have a bath. No pipe was available in those days right after the war. But it was shelter and was a comfortable little cottage well patronized for years.

As we started on the second cottage, we soon found that the pattern of the first, and our experience in building it, made the work go faster despite the fact the peak of the summer heat had arrived and the thermometer soared 8 to 12 degrees above a hundred every afternoon.

On one of the hottest afternoons in July we were resting briefly on the porch after lunch. What little breeze there was seared the skin and heat waves rising from the desert made the foliage appear to be riding on a rough sea.

A wisp of dust rose above the road where it comes into view around Dinosaur Mountain, two miles to the south. The dust was moving in our direction and, as always, we speculated who our visitor might be.

Steaming from the exertion of climbing the road, an ancient Chevy coupe heaved to below the house. One of the broadest men I had ever seen emerged from the car and with some difficulty made his way to our porch. He was an oldish man, but his difficulty in getting around seemed to be more from his size than his age.

He did not reply to our "Good afternoon," but huffed and puffed right past us into the most comfortable chair in sight, eased himself into it, coaxed a red bandana from his hip pocket and mopped his face and neck. Seconds, even minutes ticked away as he sat speechless, seeming to let his boil settle to a slow simmer. Lucy offered him a drink of water, which he gratefully accepted with a nod. We waited in silence until the shade cooled him, and at length he started looking around at the view.

Finally, pointing to the north, "Are there Indian pictures on the rocks in that canyon?"

"Yes."

"And a spring and pools of water in a large rock basin?"

"Yes."

I thought he wished he were there so he could douse himself in cool water.

"That's the place."

Another silence dragged along as the cooling off continued. Lucy and I exchanged glances but did not want to push the conversation for which the visitor obviously wished to set the pace.

"That's the place. They call it Hieroglyphic Canyon. Twenty-eight years ago during Prohibition, I had the finest still in Arizona beside that spring. It was a 25 barrel still and I made the best whiskey you ever tasted. Made a gallon of whiskey from

"When we had the picture developed we discovered something wholly unexpected. There at the foot of the left post stood Blackie on three feet, christening the sign. Bless his little black heart!" *Page 146*

Lucille Ingham King,
September 13, 1905 – March 2, 1999

Julian M. King
April 2, 1907 – November 12, 1972

"We're going West! We climbed into the '41 Ford convertible we purchased before the war, drove to Chicago and bought a travel trailer at a trade show. Everything we owned was in the little trailer which turned its face with ours toward the setting sun." *Page 13*

"After eating the dust of the Ford from coast to coast, our little trailer seemed to heave a sigh of relief as we settled it down in the shade of Quick's sprawling mesquites." *Page 22*
They swapped the trailer for 80 acres in May of 1946.

"A sprawling white frame and rock ranch house stood beneath their shade. Sheltered in a string of hills on the south and the Superstitions on the north, the place showed a feeling of timelessness and serenity, a home loved by its occupants. We felt like intruders as we opened the gate to enter the yard." *Page 17*

The ***3R*** house burned in the 1960s, leaving only one stone structure which still stood next to Apacheland Studios until it was razed in 2005 to make way for development.

Gertrude Mae Anderson Barkley
07/31/1886–07/09/1972

"We were greeted by a capable looking woman, past middle age. Her voice was strong and clear, her eyes direct, inquiring. By the time I introduced ourselves and felt the firm grasp of her strong hand, I knew she had us sized up." *Page 17 (Photos courtesy of Nancy Barkley McCollough)*

William Augustus (Tex) Barkley
08/11/1879 – 09/20/1955

"He was tall and lanky with skin like sun-parched rawhide. He wore scuffed boots and a faded shirt. A rawhide piggin' string instead of a belt was threaded though the loops of his Levi's. A battered, broad-brimmed hat sat flush with his eyebrows. Here was a cowman of the old school." *Page 17*

"Had a ballet of exotic dancers appeared before us, I think my eyes would have continued to admire that gorgeous slab of concrete. It was our first permanent mark on the broad expanse of this tremendous land." *Page 57*

"This was the first time we had ever laid one rock upon another, but again we fell back upon the old argument that we had seen people who didn't look any smarter than we building rock walls." *Page 67*

"Compared to the rock work, the carpentry went fast. In no time at all the framing was up and the rafters were clawing at the sky." *Page 97*

"The long, broad porch effectively doubled our living space. The size of the rooms did not make much difference because most of our living was out of doors anyway." *Page 129*

Paul Marchand in his living quarters

"I'm kinda hankerin' to join your outfit. I got my own bedroll and fryin' pan so I don't need a helluvamuch to get along." *Page 114*

"Whitey ran up my back and stood on top of my head. This became one of the kid's daily tricks and I didn't object unless he tried to chew my hair." *Page 85*

"Although it was a breach of the frontier way of life, we thought our guests would be grateful for the added amenities of electric lights, gas stoves, and heaters." *Page 171*

"'Miss Springbottom and I should like to spend a couple of weeks with you if you can accommodate us. We shall require two cottages with private bawth.' I swallowed twice before explaining about our private "bawth" arrangement, and was amazed when they accepted what we had." *Page 181*

The all purpose utility trailer. It hauled water, goats, burros, lumber, firewood and horses with equal dependability.

Julian and Lucy in front of residence/office

The Kings of Kings Ranch

The Kings' gracious living quarters

Mother King, Julian, Bruce King, and Lucy.

Julian and Lucy in their new home after they sold the resort. The home was featured in the Arizona Republic in May of 1961. It has been extensively remodeled, but retains the original adobe walled studio, beautiful stone fireplace and ornate gate.

Lucy King at her 93rd birthday celebration, September 13, 1998.
Alex Shearer, grandson of Rosemary and Larry Shearer, is on her lap.

Lucy King at a reunion with Kings Ranch wrangler, Paul Marchand,
at Dirtwater Springs Restaurant in Apache Junction.

January, 1999.

every ten pounds of sugar I could tote in on my burro. Had a still all made of copper, coils and everything. Made it myself. I sold whiskey to the best people in Arizona. I could sell all I made. They came for miles around to buy my likker.

"That water is the best you ever saw anywhere for making likker. I've had stills in Oklahoma and Missouri, and Pennsylvania and Georgia and everywhere, but I never had no better water than that."

"I guess you had to pack in all your food and supplies on your burros?"

"Well, yes, at first. Then I got some chickens and a fresh goat and they just did fine up there in the canyon. I had my own eggs and milk and meat and the deer and wildlife used to come to the spring so I had fresh meat about whenever I wanted it. There's lots of quail up there and they're good eatin'. And mesquite beans. Hell, the Indians made grinding holes in the rocks up there, and them ground mesquite beans are fine for a man. I got along pretty good without packing in much food. Just sugar."

"Didn't the revenuers ever bother you?"

"Oh, sure, them damn fools. They used to sit up on that hill over there," pointing southeast toward the hill behind the 3R Ranch, "and watch me through their glasses. Then they'd come over to see me. I was doin' so good, though, that I'd just go in and pay their fines and be back to my still by evening. They fined me a dozen times — usually $100, and then they gradually worked it up to $500. The $500 was a little irritatin', but the price of whiskey was good so I didn't mind too much. It was cheaper than payin' rent.

"But then one day they brought along a smart aleck revenoor from the coast. He says, 'This time we're goin' to fine you $1,000.' Well, you know, that's kinda stiff. You got to sell a lot of likker to pay them $1,000 fines. I says, 'Now look, fellas, you pushed old man Pete just once too often. I ain't agoin' to pay no $1,000. I'll pay your $500 once more, but I ain't goin' to pay no $1,000. I cain't afford it.'

"That smart aleck says, 'If you cain't pay the $1,000 you'll have to go to jail.' I says, 'Alright, I'll go to your damn jail. I just ain't agoin' to pay.'

'"He says, 'Then come on and get agoin'. We're taking you to jail.'

"I says, 'Well, I ain't agoin' right now. I got my chickens and goat to feed and my burros to take care of. If I leave my still in this here canyon somebody'll run right off with it. Everybody in the county knows I've got the best damn outfit in Arizona. No sir! I can't just take off like that.'

"Well, ya know, that set 'em back a little. They didn't figure old Pete would talk thata way. Them fellas went in a crouch and parlayed for a while. They knew damn well I'd cause 'em trouble if all them animals died on their account. Finally they come back. I was drawin' off some dew, but I stopped workin' to talk to 'em.

"The big fella, who had been to see me before said, 'Pete, we'll let you take care of your stock if you'll promise to come to jail on Tuesday.'

"'Hell, fellas,' I says, 'I cain't possibly get to jail by Tuesday. I've got to find somebody to take care of my chickens while I'm in jail, and then I've got to haul my chickens in to 'em. Then I've got to find somebody to take care of Gertrude. And then I've got to take her in. Hell, Gertrude will never give milk again if she don't get good care. And then I've got to get somebody to leave my burros with. So ya see, fellas, I cain't possibly be to jail by Tuesday.'

"That set them fellas back again. They had another parlay and come back. The big guy says, 'Okay, Pete, when can you make it?'

"If you fellas let me take care of my stuff I'll do my best. I know I can make it to jail by Friday. I'm an honest man and I'll come sooner if I can make it. You fellas know me. I'm honest and hard workin' and I never run out on you yet.'

"I guess they figgered I meant what I said, because the boss man finally says, 'Okay, Pete, you come to jail on Friday and don't make it a day later.'

"'You needn't worry a bit. And if I can make it earlier, I sure will,' I says, and them fellas went away."

Pete fell into a contemplative silence. There was a suggestion of a smile on his face. When he didn't continue, I said, "Well, I guess you made it okay by Friday?"

"Hell, on Friday I was agoin' through Kansas. They never did catch me!"

His face broke into a smile as big as a sunrise.

15

Quick and the Dutchman

BY THE TIME THE OLD MAN WAS READY TO TAKE HIS LEAVE, half the afternoon was gone. Before Pete got his car turned around, Quick Upton's old Ford rattled to a stop in the drive and he and Daisy alighted. It was hot anyhow, so we gave up work for the rest of the afternoon.

"Come on up on the porch in the shade," Lucy called. I pointed to our burlap-wrapped water jug hanging from a rafter and invited them to have a drink.

"What do you hear from Ma?" I asked, a little mischievously.

"Jeepers, King, I ain't heard from Ma and probably won't. You know she was getting a little prevokin' just before she left. I don't care if she falls for that Oregon country." Daisy listened half smiling. "But what I come over to tell you about was an old Spanish mine I run onto the other day. King, them Spaniards just touched it before the Apaches killed 'em off. Why there's gold on the walls, gold on the floor, gold on the ceiling, and it's all rich stuff. It outta run $1,000 to the ton."

We were off on another bonanza. You could count on at least one a week, even if there wasn't enough money in the house for cigarettes. Paul sat on the edge of his chair and Daisy had a look on her face that said she wished she had a few tons of that ore.

"What makes you think it's an old Spanish digging, Quick?"

"Shucks, I know a Spanish mine when I see one. Them fellers had a different way of mining. They didn't allow much headroom, for one thing, and you can tell the marks of their tools. You see, King, things was different a hunnert years ago when them fellers was in this country. Their tools wasn't exactly like ours and they didn't use 'em the same way you and I would these days. No, you can't fool old Quick about a Spanish mine, King, and that's all they are of it!"

He settled back in his chair to tell the whole story.

A hundred years ago three Spanish dons, the Peralta brothers, brought a small crew into the Superstitions. They discovered gold and took some back to Sonora, Mexico, in the spring of 1847. Two of the brothers brought out enough that they were satisfied to buy big cattle spreads and go into the cow business. But the third brother wanted more gold. That fall he organized an expedition of about 75 men and returned to the Superstitions, entering the mountains through what is now called Peralta Canyon.

"That's the entrance to Peralta Canyon right over there at the foot of that second bluff," Quick said. He pointed to the east where two cliffs rose precipitously from the desert floor against the mountains about six or eight miles away.

"They mined all that fall and winter," he continued. "The Superstitions were full of Apache who regarded the mountains as sacred. When the Spaniards started to leave the mountains in the spring, the Apaches descended on them and massacred the whole outfit except two boys, who escaped to later tell the tale. The Indians scattered the gold, covered up the diggings and even camouflaged the old mines so no one could find them. Some of the scattered gold was found later on the side of the ridge to the north."

Quick told us that in the 1870's a Dutchman by the name of Jacob Walz was in the mountains prospecting with his partner.

"One day they heard the sound of picks on rocks and crept toward the noise to see what was going on. They saw two guys mining and approached to see what they might have discovered. They had found gold. Plenty of rich ore, apparently, so old Jake and his partner just up and shot those two guys and took over the mine. They started working it and there was even more gold than they had thought at first. So old Jake just up and shot his partner, and the mine was his. Nice guy, wasn't he?"

He'd found gold all right, and brought it out to Phoenix and Florence. In the next ten years he brought out about a quarter of a million dollars worth, Quick said. People tried to follow him into the mountains. Old Jake, however, was too clever for them. He'd double back on his trail whenever he thought someone might be behind him, and bushwhack anybody in sight.

"He killed eight or ten guys who tried to follow him," Quick vowed, "but he managed to keep his secret. In 1891 he died without telling anyone where he got his gold. Julia Thomas, his housekeeper, was beside him when he died and claimed Jake told her where it was. In fact, she made up some maps and sold them for pretty good prices, but they were all phony."

"What did Walz do with his gold?"

"Just got drunk. Got drunk, stayed drunk, and kept his friends drunk just as long as the gold lasted, then he'd go back into the mountains and get another jag of gold so he could go on a spree again. That's about all he ever did with it."

"How come you never been able to find the Lost Dutchman Mine?" Paul asked.

"Jeepers, if you hang around this country long enough you'll learn just how rough them mountains is," Quick explained. "They wear out men and beasts and a man can't cover much ground in a day. I know where the Dutchman Mine is, but it's buried under an avalanche, and I never could get enough money together to move the overburden. A feller can't do it alone. He needs help. Even the guys who got the money to help either don't believe or they're not good enough men to go back into the Superstitions to see.

"Course, I located this mine by readin' the signs. I've been studyin' them for years. You see, King, them old Spaniards made symbols on rocks. They cut saguaros in ways that followers in their band could understand, and in LeBarge Canyon right on the face of the canyon wall is a whole map of their mines, but nobody but me's got the key to their map these days. Took me years to figger it all out, but by God, I done it, King. That's all they are to it.

"This old Spanish mine I've just located is the biggest find I ever made, folks, and you ought to go in with me on it. There's a fortune in it for all of us."

"No, Quick," I said, "we've got our work cut out for us right here. I know if I ever hooked up with you to go prospecting, this ranch would never amount to anything. You'll get a partner with more money than I've got and really make a fortune on this one."

I changed the subject and turned to Daisy. "You look like you're feeling a lot better, Daisy."

"Oh, I feel just fine," she beamed. "Quick got over his arthritis here and he knows all about how to do it. He tells me what to eat and what exercises to take and all that. Look how I can bend my wrists." She rotated her hands to show how she'd improved. She was able to turn her head in a wide arc without any pain, she told us.

"She'll get along just fine if she keeps letting me help her," said Quick, as he rose to leave.

We watched the pair drive down the hill.

"I wonder how Ma's fruit picking in Oregon is going," remarked Lucy.

16

Sis and the Rattlesnake

By early September we were, to our way of thinking, comfortably situated. All of the essentials had been provided and each little improvement was a cause to rejoice.

We bought another No. 7 wood-burning stove, two second-hand iceboxes and mounted another water barrel on the back wall of the house. Lucy had scraped, repaired and painted the old ice-boxes. It was handy to have one right in the kitchen. When we didn't get to town often enough for ice we used the desert cooler as a standby.

The wall in the center of the ranch house divided it into two one-room apartments. Or maybe I should call them compartments, each 12 by 20 feet. The long, broad porch effectively doubled our living space. The size of the rooms did not make much difference because most of our living was out of doors anyway, and about all we did indoors was prepare meals and change clothes.

Lucy and I had decided to rent the north half of the house and move into the south half where we had a better view of the road. Visitors were important to us, so we didn't want to miss a single one.

We were moving our belongings from the north to the south half of the house, and a new bed, tables, and furnishings into the north half when a car with a Nebraska license stopped in the yard, and out stepped Lucy's sister, Edna and her husband Harold. It was a complete surprise and we were glad to see someone from home.

It was doubly surprising to find them here, for Edna's letters had been full of misgivings about the climate ruining Lucy's hair and skin, the loneliness we were bound to suffer after our "exciting" life in the city, and the dangers constantly threatening us in the desert, particularly outlaws, scorpions — and rattlesnakes. She faithfully hoped we would get along without accident or calamity, but the chances were 60 to 40 in favor of calamity. We didn't know how Harold felt on these subjects, for he didn't write letters.

"Boy, this is sure swell country," he said as he emerged from the car. We knew where we stood with Harold right then.

"How in the name of Heaven did you find this place?" asked Edna. Before we could tell her she continued, "But it *is* really pretty out here, isn't it?"

We were encouraged.

Lucy was so glad to see her sister that there were tears in her eyes. They had not been together for four years, and although there had not been a word of it, I'm sure there were occasions of misapprehension and weariness for Lucy when it would have been heartening to be nearer the family circle. She had been toiling constantly for months, hard work she had never done before. The great wonder was that she had been able to continue without completely wearing herself out and had the will to persist in our project without complaint or discouragement. Edna's visit would be a great tonic for her and I secretly planned to see to it that Lucy didn't have a thing to do but relax and enjoy the folks.

Of course Lucy's idea of relaxing when she is with people she loves is to turn out a banquet for every meal, finding ways even with primitive equipment to cater to their individual wants, and still keep all the mechanics of everyday living running smoothly. She does all this so effortlessly you seldom notice she is busy.

This was our first such festive occasion since we came to Arizona, and Lucy did us proud. We somehow were able to toast the reunion properly, eat an enormous dinner, and settle down for the evening unaware that she had even been absent from the group or had missed a word that was said.

Summer still lay on the land and the days were hot, but in the evening the cool comes down from the mountain. Arizona summer skies are more brilliant, more spectacular even than in the southern hemisphere with its famed Southern Cross.

Gathered on the patio, under God's glorious mantle and surrounded with the magic of desert stillness, conversation flows easily. We had drifted from news of family and friends to tales of our guest-ranch venture and life in our new surroundings. Edna is somewhat on the conservative side and a bit skeptical of anything done differently than it is done in Omaha, but she seemed pleased that we were so enthusiastic, and admitted we had made more progress than she thought possible. Our life seemed at least a little less rugged than she had envisioned.

We spun the evening full of yarns as bedtime sneaked up on us. Sleeping under the stars is to us one of the great thrills of life on the desert, and with the full moon making the night half as light as day, Harold was easily sold.

"Won't that be great, Edna?" he said.

Edna grew pale. "Out here? With the rattlesnakes?"

"You don't have to worry about rattlesnakes," assured Lucy. "There are a few around, but a rattlesnake is a gentleman if you let him be, and will always rattle if you give him a chance. We respect them, but don't really fear them. We've only run across four since we came to the ranch. They rattled and we killed all four. Haven't seen one in more than a month. The cats and Blackie keep them away."

With a shudder Edna said, "I don't know what I would do if I heard one. I think I'd just pass out!"

I added to Lucy's assurances that there was nothing to worry about, and finally, with obvious misgivings she agreed to join us. We set up a double folding bed for them, just off the edge of the porch where they too could enjoy the evening coolness which dripped through the millions of star holes in the sky. All of us fell asleep quickly.

An hour after midnight I felt a tug at my toe. It was Lucy.

"There's a rattlesnake around somewhere," she whispered.

"How do you know?"

"Goldie and Blackie are acting funny and I think I hear it."

I got out of bed as noiselessly as possible, put on my slippers, and started looking for the little intruder who had the gall to make us first class liars. Harold had heard the disturbance and now joined us. I whispered an explanation. He too was clad in slippers and pajamas.

By this time Blackie had found the rattler under a bush not ten feet from the foot of Edna's bed. The dog had the sense to keep just beyond the snake's striking distance. It could do nothing but sit coiled in striking position as long as Blackie's barking was a threat. I picked up a rock the size of a small watermelon, dropped it on the snake, and he stopped his noise. When I had examined the remains to be sure he would bother us no longer, Harold and I started back to bed. As we turned, we noticed Edna.

She sat, bolt upright, quivering in the center of the bed, huddled into as little space as her 140 pounds would permit. Hands covered her face, and through them sobs abused the silence and tranquility of the moonlit desert.

In a quavering voice supercharged with dread she ventured, "Is that horrible thing dead?"

We assured her that is was very dead.

"Then take it away — a long ways away. Oh, I never want to go through this again. I thought surely both of you boys would be killed. Out here in the desert in your pajamas and slippers with no light." She continued to quake. "I'm scared to death!"

A little conversation was calming, before long the worst of the storm was over, and Edna lay down again. I don't think she relaxed the rest of the night, but her actions and reactions seemed normal in the morning, despite her violent introduction to the desert.

Before the week was over it started to rain. Edna and Harold were in for another desert surprise. It rained steadily for three days and three nights, almost six inches in total. The desert is not accustomed to water in such quantities. For the first time water could be heard roaring in the ordinarily dry wash some 300 yards from the house, and rivulets formed everywhere.

The face of the Superstitions was streaked with long, slender waterfalls which persisted for two days. The heavy rains had brought frogs out of hibernation and they could be heard croaking as though we were beside a marsh. We saw two desert tortoises nearly a foot in diameter.

Our house withstood this unusual test and it felt good to know we had built it so well. The yard, however, had not been graded to shed this much water and we were out in the rain with shovels to ditch along the uphill side of the house to keep water from the back doors. The graveled floor of the front porch was not sloped for drainage and now was almost a lake.

We were learning.

There was a small island near the wall, and here the dog and two cats were marooned, Blackie lying on his side with both kittens cuddled close to his chest for warmth. They were rescued and put in the house beside the wood-burning stove which glowed in welcome warmth.

Rain fills the air with a fragrance which belongs to the desert alone. A dark green bush called creosote, grows profusely. The Indians and ranchers of early days used it for medicinal tea and

poultices. When rains wash the brilliant leaves, the creosote bush gives off a pungent perfume with just a touch of the odor its name implies, but pleasant and rather surprising because of its unexpectedness. The sage brush emits a fresh, herbal scent. The gently scented mesquite blossoms attract bees which, if you can find their hives, provide a delicious honey. The Indians found their beans handy for making flour, and they provide wonderful shade. In lesser ways the other growth and, indeed, the earth, share their freshness and encouragement with all who walk in the desert and partake of it.

At dusk of the third day the sun poked through the western clouds and cast against the waterfall-streaked face of the Superstitions an unbelievable double rainbow of startling brilliance. Had an artist caught the colors on canvas they would have seemed garish.

The storm was gone the fourth day, and the sun shone brightly. It was warm again but not so warm as before the rain. The desert had a scrubbed look about it. The foliage was greener, the air was clearer, and the moist ground had a darker, richer look. It had been a refreshing, cleansing flow of moisture from which the cactus would drink in and store its water reserve for the dry months to come. The fall grass would thrive on this rare gorge of moisture. All animals, wild and domestic, would flourish on the more abundant food, and to the cattleman it was manna from Heaven.

We told Edna and Harold all we could about the desert. Edna was interested in the people, the visitors, and in visitors' reactions to the ranch. Harold was interested in rocks, animals, birds, gold, cowboys and any evidence of the old-time West he'd read about so often.

As though Providence had sent him to give Edna a first-hand experience with one of our unusual callers, we all were awakened about 6:00 a.m. the fifth morning of their visit by a man who strode onto our terrace and shouted to the four sleeping forms, "HEY. Where's the Superstition Mountain?"

Lucy was closest to him. She raised her head from the pillow and shook it in an effort to clear this strange face from her eyes, as though she might be seeing it in a dream. But the face was still there and it said, "I've been looking for Superstition Mountain for an hour and half now. Where is it?"

Lucy sat bolt upright, glared at him, and pointed north. "If you'll look in that direction all you can see is Superstition Mountain. If you look close, you'll see the Lost Dutchman Mine. What's the idea of going around peeking at people at this time of day, anyhow?"

I'm pretty foggy on awakening in the morning, but by now I was beginning to come around and found myself unconsciously reaching for the .30-.30 which lay on the ground under my bed.

"That ain't Superstition Mountain! I saw it in 1944, and that ain't the same mountain! Where is it at? Superstition Mountain's got holes in it and you can see clear back into the canyons."

"Look, Mister, I'm telling you that that's Superstition Mountain. Now go away and let us sleep."

My wife does not suffer fools gladly.

"What kind of a place is this, anyhow?" the stranger asked.

"It's a ranch."

"People sure pick funny places to put ranches."

My fingers closed around the .30-.30.

"Mister," Lucy said with emphasis, "just go back down the road two miles and take the left fork and drive up to the mountain so you can see it better."

Our ranch is perched at the very foot of this magnificent mountain, and you needed to duck to see the top out of our front windows if you were standing inside.

"I just wanted to show my wife and daughter Superstition Mountain, but we ain't got time to go looking around any more. Got to be back in Hollywood tonight."

I broke in. "For Heaven's sake, go away and let us sleep. Otherwise I'll let the air out of your tires with this popgun of mine."

He beat a hasty retreat.

"Thanks for showing me Superstition Mountain," he said as he jumped into his car. The engine roared and the car disappeared down the road in a cloud of dust.

"Put that .30-.30 up and go back to sleep. Don't you know that gun's loaded?"

"You're darn right it's loaded. What good would it be if it weren't?"

"I see what you mean about strange callers," laughed Edna.

By the time they left at the end of the week Edna had recovered from her first experience with a rattlesnake and was just beginning to feel at ease in the desert. She saw beauty in the sunsets, the mountains, and other living things. We have often thought that she would have gotten sand in her shoes in another week or so.

Harold's enthusiasm bloomed until he could hardly contain himself. The only time I noticed it slip was when he came to the house with my shotgun over his shoulder, and with a broad, proud smile on his face, started to hand me a jack rabbit he had shot.

I failed to reach for the rabbit as he had expected and instead, remarked, "Part of the pleasure of hunting is in skinning out your own game."

Harold took the hint, got the skinning knife down from the back door jamb and went to work. We had rabbit for supper and he was as proud as though he had brought in venison.

Their visit had been such fun that the desert seemed a little empty when they left. So many things demanded doing, however, that we had little time to be lonesome. The Fall Visitor Season was almost upon us.

17

Father and Mother Try the Desert

ONE VANITY SHARED BY MOST HUMANS is the desire to have family members understand, approve, and — most glorious of all — envy us our status of living.

Lucy's and my decision to abandon an excellent job and luxuriant living in New York to hack out a meager existence in what seemed to most relatives as a God-forsaken corner of the earth, brought varied reactions.

Lucy's mother could understand our reasoning and the satisfaction we were deriving from our new way of life because she and Mr. Ingham had broken new sod in Texas, Iowa, and Nebraska. She had planned to visit us as soon as the house was built, but her health failed quickly and she was unable to realize that dream. Lucy's brothers, Leroy and Lloyd were never surprised at anything their Sis decided to do, and our settling in the desert was okay by them. They'd worry more about Lucy bothering the rattlesnakes than vice versa. Edna now could assure them that the ratio for our survival had reversed and we might have a 60 to 40 chance.

My parents, on the other hand, were too stunned to comprehend. Their early life in Colorado and Nebraska brought them friendly understanding of outdoor people, but they never could share our devotion to land, space or Nature. When father was called into Washington, D.C. in 1934 as an expert on grain marketing, he and Mother melted into Capitol life as naturally as if they had been born there. To them it was inconceivable that their son, their own flesh and blood, could develop a sense of values so contrary to their own. They were convinced the shock of war had unbalanced us, had driven us to throwing away our education and our lives. What else could have carved such a chasm between them and in our thinking?

To them, city life was a well-oiled, bump-free existence of culture, intelligent conversation, "civilized" conventions, dictated by people who knew only the "right way" of doing things. To us, city life was strangling. It exemplified smoke-filled offices and nightclubs, noise, subways, wrangling over dollars, stuffy bridge parties, never mind who you trample — just get ahead and stay ahead by outwitting competitors. All of these factors bruised our souls and numbed our thinking.

It was hard to put these thoughts into letters. We were trying to convey to them not only the beauty of our mountains and trees and the captivating wonder of all the strange things that grow in the Sonoran desert, but also the peace that emanates from space and silence, the freedom from constraint in your thinking; the reawakening of your awareness that you are an individual.

Apparently I wasn't making too much headway, for to them the desert was a barren wasteland of sand, rocks, stickers, heat, rattlesnakes, dust and loneliness.

I've never been able to resist teasing Mother, and one of her most vulnerable characteristics is her affinity for emergencies. She can't relax until she has anticipated every conceivable disaster and marked out a solution for each. That we lived *miles* from telephone, telegraph or neighbors practically guaranteed calamity, and her letters showed increasing concern. In reply to an urgent plea that she must know how to reach us in case of emergency, I gave her an answer that was truthful, but designed to make her sputter:

"Telegraph or telephone the Sheriff's office and request he send a posse with the message to the southwest quarter of Section 33, Township One North, Range 9 East of the Gila and Salt River Meridian."

Whether it was this evidence of barbaric existence that catapulted Mother into the conviction that she was *needed* out here or whether our campaign to sell them on desert life had finally melted their most frozen resistance, I couldn't tell. But September brought the welcome news they were coming for a visit.

A million odds and ends were crying for attention in order that we might get ready for guests. Two biffys, better than the airy ocotillo throne we had inherited from Pearly Bates, would have to be installed in back of the new cottages. Water pipe for the modern conveniences to come later just wasn't in the market at any price in these early years after the war. There must be drainage for waste water from the sinks. More second-hand stoves and iceboxes must be bought, reconditioned and installed. All the cottages must be shellacked. There was furniture to be built, screen doors to install, beds and chairs to purchase, floors to finish and oil, yards to clean, scrap lumber to be gathered and cut into stove wood, water barrels must be installed on each cottage, steps put to the front doors... There seemed to be no limit to the demands of our time and pocketbook.

Then something really should be done about attracting guests. We couldn't just wait for people to find us clear up here in the desert, or we'd starve.

In the evenings I worked on a brochure for our guest ranch. We had puzzled about a name. Spanish is commonly understood in this country and arty names woven of Spanish words are popular. We toyed with the idea of using the Spanish equivalent of Kings Ranch — *"El Rancho del Reyes."* It was no good. People would call it "Kings Ranch" no matter what words we might use. We'd just as well call it that and be done with it. Yet it was not to be a ranch in the sense that we ran cattle or raised crops. It was in the country, so "Kings Ranch Resort" seemed appropriate and honest, and that was put on the rough sketch of our new folder.

A sign was needed on the highway where our three-mile road left the pavement. We went to an advertising company and arranged for a double-faced sign, 5 feet by 8, to be set up at the junction of two roads.

My parents were expected to arrive on Tuesday evening. Lucy and I were determined to make the folks as comfortable as possible, feed them well and induce them to like our desert, so we went to town earlier that day to restock our larder.

They fooled us. Proceeding under forced draft they had shortened their elapsed time to a near record, and when we returned to the ranch at noon, here were my mother and father sitting on the porch.

They were disappointed that no reception committee was on hand, and we were chagrined that we had not been home to make their arrival a gala affair. But they arrived safely, found us without trouble and now were in good spirits.

We had an old-fashioned family reunion. They had examined everything and found us more comfortable than seemed possible. Mother was particularly observant on matters of detail. Small things which we had taken for granted and considered of little or no importance had been noted and received her tearful approval. In fact she admitted having cried over each evidence of our grueling work.

Both were amazed that the desert was not as they had imagined. Trees actually grew here, the cactus wasn't productive, but it did cover the ground with green, and the mountains in the background actually were as beautiful as we had said. Father thought it would be better if the mountains could have been covered with pines like those in Colorado. They weren't quite right without those pine trees, but the many colors in the rocks and

the green brush in the canyons did produce a beautiful, though different, landscape.

We moved the folks into the north half of our house, had lunch, and spent the remainder of the day showing them around and explaining our plans and expectations. By evening they did not see us quite as demented as we had seemed from the pinnacle of Washington, D.C.

Lucy and I wanted more than anything that they should like our new home. Father would retire before long and we quietly hoped they would come live on the ranch. It would be fun for us all and a good life for them, away from the bedlam of the city in the most beautiful climate ever found.

Father was wearing his business clothes. White shirt, polka dot bow tie, Panama hat and meticulously clean black and white sport oxfords. His white silk socks with black clocks were a favorite touch of elegance. Mother was in a tailored suit with fluffy silk blouse, broad brimmed hat with flowers, and shoes entirely inappropriate to the desert.

I told Lucy, "Watch Dad tomorrow. We won't say anything about the tie and white shirt, but I kind of think they will come off soon. And the first morning he forgets to shave, we're in!"

Father had never appeared anywhere unshaven, to my knowledge, in all my thirty-eight years.

The next morning we had breakfast together on the front porch. It was arranged as part of our attack. The warm morning sun, the beauty of the Superstitions, the limitless expanse of desert to the south, all combined to conquer the most adamantine soul. There was a gentle breeze, the cottontail rabbits and quail were busying about their routine visits for food and water when Lucy set out the coffee pot and invited us to sit down. The aroma of the coffee in the fresh morning air brought all of us to the table at once.

The folks were up early and in fine fettle after resting well. Lucy served up a breakfast of ham, eggs, fried potatoes, juice and toast that would have started anyone's day right. Mother and Father enjoyed picnics and this breakfast in the early morning sun suited them to a T. It was a good beginning.

Father was wearing an old pair of shoes and trousers, but still wore a white shirt and polka dot bow tie.

"We know you have a lot to do," he said, "and we don't want to interfere in any way. In fact, we came to help, so if you have some little job I can do, just put me to it."

He was Lucy's pigeon. She had undertaken the chore of varnishing the cottages, and this was a project on which she really could use Dad's help. She took him into her crew like a vacuum cleaner grabs a toothpick, and the morning work started shortly after breakfast.

"I'm no good at painting or building, but I'll do the dishes and the housework so Lucy can get out and boss Father," Mother offered. "I'll get lunch and take care of any mending or washing you may have to do."

What she offered was a great help, and we gladly accepted. She pitched in with a will, undeterred by our lack of conveniences to which she was accustomed. Most of our clothes needed mending, for we'd been working in high gear and Lucy had no time for details, so Mother's help with needle and thread was an unexpected boon.

I watched Father work. His white sleeves were rolled above his wrists, but the bow tie and Panama hat remained as trim as ever throughout the day. At supper time Lucy pronounced him a good hand. He'd kept right on the job and covered more than his share of the surfaces with shellac. We knocked off a little earlier than usual, in deference to our hard-working guests.

"Where's the shower bath?" Dad was hot and thirsty.

"Right beside the pump. Bring your towel and come along with me and I'll start the pump. Lucy, you keep Mother here on the porch so Dad can have privacy." I started off in the direction of the pump.

"Well — uh — that is, do you mean down there on that little slab of concrete?"

"Sure. That's our shower. I'll hold the hose for you."

"Well, yes, I know, but suppose a car should come up the road. It's only a hundred feet from the road."

"There won't be any cars."

"Nope. I will not do that. I'll take a bath out of that wash pan I saw under the sink this morning. You don't get me out there all stark naked before the whole world."

Our shower had been spurned.

The next morning found us on the porch for breakfast again. Mother had gotten the lay of the land by now and helped Lucy with preparations. If anything, it was an even more beautiful morning than the day before.

Dad was minus the bow tie and had donned an older shirt, opened at the neck.

We and the desert were making progress.

"What's on the program today, Son?"

"I've plenty of work on my list, but I don't suppose I could get you out of the painting gang."

"No, sir," put in Lucy. "He's my assistant and you can't have him. Pop, we've still got about a day's varnishing and then that job is done."

The next morning Dad forgot to shave. The shirt was open at the throat, and in place of the Panama, Father was wearing an old cap he had carried in the car for years just in case he had to get out and crawl under. His hair was snow white and he always protected it well.

The desert was gaining ground.

On the appointed day Father and I towed the trailer to town, took delivery of our sign, loaded some new lumber, half a dozen sacks of cement, groceries, ice and miscellaneous purchases. By noon we were home again, anxious to erect the sign, our first announcement to the public that there was a guest ranch at the foot of fabled Superstition Mountain and it was open for business.

Paul and I dug post holes, set deadmen, erected the sign and guyed it to the deadmen with barbed wire. It was a workmanlike job and we stood off, the better to see our handiwork. It was satisfying. We got into the car and drove down the road, approaching it from each side as a winter visitor might. The sign could be read from some distance, and looked inviting. We were all proud of the public launching of our new enterprise.

"Let's take a picture of Julian and Lucy in front of the new sign," Mother suggested. "It is your first and I want a photo for our book."

It was a good picture, but when we had it developed we discovered something wholly unexpected. There at the foot of the left post stood Blackie on three feet, christening the sign. Bless his little black heart!

The next day after work, Father said to me, "Son, let's look around a little bit. I don't suppose it will ever happen, but someday we just might want to build a little home out here for the winter, and I'd like to see if you have a suitable place."

This was it! Lucy overheard the suggestion and gave me a broad wink. As sure as taxes our wish was coming true.

Already Lucy and I had decided privately that in the event this should happen, the site where our trailer had been parked would be a suitable one. Father and I went to examine it.

"There is a fine view from here," I pointed out. "You can see Randolph Canyon, the full sweep of the Superstitions, and that long, hundred-mile view to the south is one you'll particularly enjoy. At first it doesn't seem as spectacular as the view of the mountains, but you'll find your eyes spending more and more time on it."

Father was definitely interested. "Do you think you can supply us with water from your well?"

I assured him that it would be simple to run a waterline through the lot when we installed pipe, put in a tee and he'd be in business.

"You know, this really *is* pretty here. The palo verdes will shield us from the road, the drive could come around past the trees, through here, alongside the house." He started designing the front yard, mentally planting flowers, building rock walls.

"Now you understand," he turned to me gravely, "this may never happen. I'm just looking the ground over while we're here, just in case."

The Bateses had returned from Springerville early in September before the summer heat had left the desert and a month earlier than they had planned in the spring. We had noticed the trailer parked under a shelter not far from Apache Junction.

Now, Mother has always been interested in people. The entire family used to laugh about Mother's experience on Washington buses, for she seemed to talk to everyone and to arrive home with their entire family histories.

"I met the most fascinating man on the bus today," she'd begin. "He is a hotbed hooker…"

"A what?" we all howled.

"A hotbed hooker. Lucy, you know what a hotbed hooker is, don't you?"

"Sounds to me like a sailor with a 48-hour pass."

"Now, Lucy, that's awful. This man told me a hotbed hooker is the person who puts a hook in a foundry furnace and pulls out a hot bed of coals. He works at the Navy foundry and they have a lot of hotbed hookers over there."

As usual, she'd found out all about the guy. "His folks live in Peewaukee, Wisconsin, and he went to high school there but the family couldn't afford to send him to college so he had to go to work. He's got a wife and two married daughters. The oldest married daughter lives in Patchogue, Long Island, and they have a son and daughter. The little boy has a black and white female dog which just had a litter of five puppies, two males and three females…."

Her interest in people brought her to wonder about Mr. and Mrs. Bates, of whom we had written at length. "I'd like to meet them," she said.

"Let's go see them," I said, and we got in the car.

Pearly was standing under the shelter when we arrived. He made no move to greet us. Ma was in the trailer. When she heard our voices, she came out the front door, a welcoming smile on her face.

I made introductions. Pearly said, "Hullo," and didn't move from his tracks. Mrs. Bates was most hospitable and turning to offer us chairs, recalled the cold fact that only one stood in the yard. It was a big, comfortable one, obviously the sole property of the old man. Mrs. Bates could sit on the trailer step if she had to sit down.

"Pa, I've been trying to get you to unpack those new chairs all summer and you wouldn't do it. Now you just go and unpack them so the Kings can sit down."

Untrue to form, Pearly responded to his wife's command and brought three new canvas-backed chairs from the storage compartment. Mrs. Bates rustled a box for me and we all sat down, with her perched on the trailer step.

"Pa was so mad by the time he got to Springerville he wouldn't unpack these chairs. He wouldn't fish. He wouldn't even talk. We never spent a worse summer."

"What in the world happened?" I asked.

"That goddam trailer of yours," snorted Pearly, "was all right in flat country but all hell broke loose when we started up the mountain."

Mother winced at the old man's language, and Father looked the other way. Both were fervent Methodists, unaccustomed to such outbursts. But Mother had wanted to meet the Bateses, so here we were.

Everything had gone fine until they started up the steep grade between Superior and Miami, Pearly said. It was a steep pull for any car, but the ton or so of treasured tools Pearly had insisted on loading in the trailer was too much. Half way up the first mountain pass the car engine got so hot the pistons stuck on the cylinders. The car stalled. The weather was hot, the engine was hot, Pa was hot, and Mrs. Bates was looking for shade at the side of the road.

Pearly left his wife to guard his tools and hitchhiked to Superior where he hired a garage man to tow his car into town and overhaul it again. Then he got a truck to tow the trailer to Springerville. Not another foot would he haul it with his own car.

"That goddam trailer cost me $175.00 to get to Springerville," he said. "Never had such a goddam summer in my life. Hell, I didn't even go fishin'. Just sat in the shade. The flies were terrible. Why, the goddam fools who built that road ought to be hung. The car was all right — I overhauled it just before we left — but that goddam road. Hell, those guys didn't know how to build a road any way but straight up."

Mother was growing more and more uncomfortable and, for once, speechless. She was squirming in her chair and looked as though she'd rather be someplace else.

I changed the subject. "You seem comfortable here."

"I guess it's not too bad, but I don't like it." Pa's pipe was swinging from the pivot on his lower jaw. "When we first parked here the goddam dogs squirted the wheels of my car morning, noon and night, but I fixed 'em. See what I done?"

He pointed to semi-circles of cholla cactus balls around each wheel.

"They get a hell of a surprise now when they come around here to pee!" He puffed up with pride at having conquered the dogs. "But that goddam zoo down there at the Junction, they got to keep their animals in cages if they want to have a zoo. The other day a monkey got loose and came down here. I shot him right between the eyes with my .45. He won't bother none of us no more."

"Well, you seem to have things pretty well under control

here. I think we'd better be on our way. We've work to do at home," I said as we started to leave.

Mrs. Bates hurried over to Lucy. "I'm so grateful to you folks for this fine trailer," she said. "It is the most wonderful, convenient home I've had in many, many years. I'm so happy here."

We took our leave. When we were on our way, Mother said, "Mercy, does everybody out here use that sort of language?"

That was our last visit with Mr. and Mrs. Bates. He died a short time later, Mrs. Bates sold the car and trailer and returned to her family in Massachusetts.

That evening Mother said, "Now you kids..." Lucy and I always flinched a little when referred to as "kids." But to Mother and Father we probably always would be kids.

"Now you kids have been working hard for long hours a good many months and you need a rest. While we're here to take care of the place you get in your car and take a little trip, just for a change. Father and I will get along just fine."

Yes, a change would be refreshing. We barely could spare the time but finally decided, with proper urging from the folks, to accept the invitation of some friends to use their mountain cottage for a few days. It was cool and comfortable there and we could lie around, read, hike or do whatever we wished. I told Paul he could take some time off and go to town. He welcomed this idea so we all took off Friday morning. Lucy and I put Paul on a bus headed west to Phoenix, then we drove to the

east. Father agreed to meet Paul's bus at 6:30 on Sunday night and Lucy and I promised to return the same evening.

We had a wonderful time in the mountains. After a summer in the desert the crisp air was refreshing and the chilly nights under blankets were like living in another world. Sunday afternoon we started home, hoping that all had gone well with Mother and Father. We were anxious that no emergencies would spoil their growing warmth toward desert living.

It was just about dusk when we approached the ranch. I could see a dim light swinging along the road about two hundred yards below the house. When we got close enough we could see it was Mother with a lantern.

"What in the (hell, I wanted to say) — What in heaven's name are you doing in the road with that lantern?" I asked her.

She was thoroughly upset. Her eyes were red and she wouldn't let her gaze leave the south where the road from the highway wandered through the desert.

"Father has been gone for more than an hour. He went to meet Paul, and should have been back long ago. I'm afraid something has happened to him." Tears had started.

"Now Mother," I spoke in a fatherly way, "you must never do a thing like this again. Chances are the bus was late, Father is waiting for it to arrive and will be home any minute. It is three miles to the highway. If you made it all the way out there, you couldn't do any good. There is a chance you'd turn an ankle or fall in the dark on the way. You must promise never to try such a foolish thing again."

"I guess you're right," she sobbed. "I'll just thrash Father when he gets home for being so late!"

The tears had disappeared and were replaced by a promise that Father was in for discipline. In a few minutes they arrived.

"Paul missed the first bus and so I waited for the second," he explained. It was so simple that Mother's reproach vanished and she went into the house for a cold root beer. Her first terrible experience in the desert had ended, with little drama and no calamities.

With Father's help, real strides had been made in finishing the buildings and they were nearly ready for occupancy. Mother had completed nearly a year's darning and mending. Our clothes again were in good condition, and the folks could take their departure with conviction that we would survive.

The desert was entwining their imaginations in its tendrils and the idea that our project was a good one had taken root. Had we been able to assure them and ourselves of financial success I think the conversion would have been completed then and there. Such was not possible, however, for the business future was uncertain and there was all too little precedent by which to judge. That would have to develop, and all of us knew it would not be too easy for a few years, at least until Kings Ranch Resort was well and favorably known to a great many more people.

We bid them goodbye and good luck. As their car started to move, we saw for the first time that our desert cats, Goldie and Brucie, were stowing away for the big city, curled up on the shelf behind the car seat. We stopped the car and retrieved our pets and offered another round of goodbyes.

As their car once again moved down the winding desert road we stood on the porch and waved until they disappeared. We could see Mother's and Father's arms waving back from the car windows until they rounded the last curve.

We felt alone and not a little lonesome.

18

Lousecake Joins the Family

As MID-OCTOBER OF 1947 ROLLED AROUND, Paul and I went to work on the third and last guest cottage we planned to build that season. Lucy turned to with determination on her job of finishing the varnish work, putting up curtains and a final cleaning of the two cottages.

Visitors dropped by so often it was difficult to get in a full day's work, and it was no surprise when Quick and Daisy drove into the yard. Quick and Ma had been so hospitable to us and generous with their water, however, that we did not mind dropping our work to greet them.

A large pile on the top of Quick's car containing pack saddles, pack boxes and harness piqued my curiosity.

"Ma ain't comin' back, King, and Daisy and me are going to get married," he said, almost the moment they got out of the car. "Daisy'd rather live in town so I won't be needin' this pack gear no more, that's all they are to it."

He walked to the side of the car and started to unload the gear. "I've prospected for a good many years but now it looks like my prospectin' days are over, so I brought all my gear to sell you."

He seemed positive he had done just what I wanted.

I thought I noted in his speech and manner a touch of remorse over giving up his free and easy life as a prospector to move to town. I couldn't picture Quick living happily in a city, even with the young lady he had chosen as his next wife. But clearly, this subject was not what was on his mind. He wanted to talk about saddles.

"I don't have any horses or burros on the place," I said, "so I don't really need those things now. I've got my hands full finishing our buildings."

"Sure, I know. But you'll have horses before long and you'll need this gear to pack folks back into the Superstitions. This is all good stuff, so I'm going to sell it to you."

Nothing would shake his confidence.

"How much do you want?"

"I'll take $20.00 for the whole outfit. There are three pack saddles, four panniers, three lash cinches, and half a dozen saddle pads. All good stuff."

By this time everything was unloaded from the top of his car and set out as though the transaction were completed. Actually it was a good deal, for in the back of my mind had always been the expectation that we would have horses, good ones, and would run pack trips into the Superstitions.

"Okay, it's a deal," I said, and handed Quick the $20.00. Had we any animals to put under these things, they were a bargain at any price. Paul's face lit up as he handled the equipment.

"I've prospected all over these hills for a good many years," said Quick as he sat down on one of the pack boxes. "Had a lot of fun and found a little mineral, but never enough to make it pay. Just enough to keep me going as hard as I could. Gonna change my life now, and move to town."

"Have you checked out that vein in Hieroglyphic Canyon?" I asked.

"Sure, me and my pardner spent a week or more in that canyon several years ago. There's a hematite vein and some fellows mined it long time ago, but if you go down a ways in the old shaft you'll find it pretty well pinches out. That's the way with a lot of the showings in this country. I always figured that the old Dutchman found a pocket or maybe several pockets of high-grade. He didn't pack much weight, you know, but there was always a lot of gold in his load."

I offered Quick a cigarette as he continued. "I'll tell you something funny that happened while we were in Hieroglyphic Canyon. One night real late we was waked up by the damnedest roar you ever heard. The whole canyon was full of noise, bouncing from one side to the other and back and forth from hell to breakfast. Me and my pardner was honest-to-God scared. Seemed like the whole mountain was going to rumble right down on top of us, rock, boulders, cactus and everything. Got up, went out and looked around, but couldn't see anything unusual. There wasn't any rocks on the move, the air was still, and the trees wasn't even waving around. But still that awful noise. It lasted several minutes then quit and the night was as quiet as any you ever seen. Not a rock had moved. I looked at my watch and it was 1:35 in the morning.

"Well, you know, that puzzled me. If I'd been alone I might have thought I'd slipped my cinch a little. But my pardner heard the same things I did and was just as scared. We fretted about that all day, and all the next day, trying to figure what had happened. Sounded like all the devils in hell was rolling rocks down the side of that canyon.

"Well, King, you know when I got home I happened to look at some newspapers a guy left in my camp and what do you suppose I ran across, all by accident. I run across a piece which said that at 1:30 that same morning there had been a lot of rock and earth slides in the mountains clear over by Globe, fifty miles from where we was. You know, that noise traveled all that ways through the rocks and come to the surface in that canyon where we was camped." He pointed to the north to the yawning entrance of Hieroglyphic Canyon.

"You know there's lots of funny things about this country. One of 'em is the way sound travels. Travels further and clearer here than anywhere I've been. Until that business up in the canyon I hadn't thought about it for years, but an old cowboy told me a story along the same lines many, many years ago when I first come to this country. You interested? I don't want to take your time if you're busy."

The fact was, we had plenty of work to do, but half the pleasure of living in the desert is the liberty to drop everything in favor of a good yarn.

"You go right ahead. We have lots of time."

"Well, this old boy had been a cowboy in his younger days and worked the range down around Picacho Peak. That's Picacho you can see off there to the south towards Tucson. That big peak — looks like a frog. Well he claimed that one night him and his pardner was camped in the desert on the lower bank of a dry warsh. The other bank was ten or twelve feet higher. During the night he was waked up by the sound of a stage coach. It was back in them days, ya see. Said he could hear the hooves of the four horses as plain as if they was right on the upper bank of the warsh.

"Him and his pardner looked. It was a moonlight night, but they couldn't see nothin', not even no dust. Them horses was in a fast trot. Then they heard the driver holler 'Whoa' and could hear other voices. There was several men and one woman. The woman was talking in Spanish and they heard the driver answer her in Spanish. These old cowboys could understand the lingo, and he said that after the stagecoach stopped he could hear this woman 'hello' a man in Spanish. He was her lover, it seemed like. It sounded just like they was throwing their arms around each other and kissing, and then you'd hear them talking. 'I could understand every word they said,' he told me."

Quick crushed his cigarette butt with his foot and ground it into the sand. "Well, King, you know that old boy and his pardner went up on the high bank and looked for tracks in the moonlight. They couldn't see a thing. In the morning they rode all around the desert and couldn't find a wheel mark, or any track or sign of teams or a human being. He said he never could prove it, but was always plumb certain that somewhere a long ways off that stagecoach had come to a stop and that Spanish couple had met, because both him and his pardner had heard it all. His pardner was as sure as he was. Said he'd heard sound travel a long ways in the desert, but that was the damnedest thing he ever heard.

"You just watch, King, and you'll see that sometimes you'll be fooled by the way the sound travels in this old desert."

Now that we're on the subject, I'm going to mention an incident which occurred about four months later, right here on the ranch, confirming Quick's stories. We had guests in the three small cottages and in the north half of our duplex. One morning I went to the cottages to see how everyone was getting along, and found the guests in conference.

It seems that about 2:30 in the morning guests in two of the cottages had heard, quite distinctly, every word of a conversation between two men, who they believed to be not further than 25 feet from their west windows. They pointed to the trees near their cottage. Both couples had gotten out of bed quietly and looked out their west windows, but could not see anyone, nor detect any movement in the trees. We were all mystified, and the women were a little afraid. Strange men in the middle of the desert close to their cottages in the dead of night did not seem too healthy.

I examined the open ground carefully for fresh tracks but could find not the slightest sign of intruders. Nothing had been disturbed anywhere and no one else had heard anything strange. We puzzled about it quietly all day and that evening. The next morning in conversation with Paul the answer came to light.

He and the son of a couple who were visiting us slept on the ground every night. Their bedrolls were spread in a little camp down near the corral, over a thousand feet from the cottages. During the night the younger man, who had asthma, suffered an attack and had to sit up. Paul awoke and started a fire, put on a coffee pot and they had talked quietly over coffee a half hour or more, then had gone back to sleep. When I questioned him closely, Paul could recollect the time, and it was the same time as the disturbance which had been reported by our guests.

An odd current of air, temperature inversion, or some unusual circumstance had carried the conversation of the two boys over this considerable distance and aroused the guests.

Since then we have had many opportunities to note these odd phenomena of the desert. They are most likely to occur when there is moisture in the air, and during the night when there are normally no other sounds.

While Quick was telling his story, Paul was going over every detail of the equipment. As soon as they left he said, "Some of this stuff needs repairs. I've got some leather scraps and rivets down to my camp and I guess I better go work this stuff over."

"Now look here, young sprout," said Lucy, "you take that stuff down and store it in your shelter, then you come right back up here and go to work with Julian. We're going to need this cottage a long time before we need riding gear."

Having blocked his escape, Lucy went back to work, Paul carried the gear to his camp and, true to orders, came back to work. In the evenings following he cut leather, riveted, and in a few days had all the equipment in passable condition. But his mind wasn't on carpentry. It was on horses. Three or four days later he made a proposal.

"Sunday when I was in town I saw Casey Wertz and he told me he had a string of horses and dude saddles he'd rent us real cheap. We could get 'em for not a helluvamuch. Pretty good outfit, too. I can put up a corral down here — I already got all the post holes marked out — and we'll be set for pack trips and everything."

I told Paul it looked like tough sledding to make any money with horses until we had a better start, but matters of business were of no interest to Paul or any other cowboy I've ever met. I'm a soft touch for anything that looks like fun, and I felt myself slipping. I had ridden often as a boy and during summers when I worked at Colorado resorts. I liked horses and it was undeniable that we'd want some as soon as we had folks to ride them.

Before you could see the bottom of the third cup of coffee my resistance had vanished and we were making a partnership agreement under which I would finance the operation and Paul would share in the earnings, if any. Paul didn't much care about the earnings if he could live here and have a string of horses. So we embarked on a new business.

Before the day was over we had seen Casey, arranged the lease of a dozen horses and saddles. I delivered Paul and his saddle to the pasture north of Phoenix where he was to pick up the animals and herd them cross-country the 50 miles to the ranch.

Neither of us actually had seen the horses. Casey allowed as how they were all top notch and was convincing enough that we tentatively leased the string, sight unseen. Now that we looked them over they did seem pretty fair.

"Any of these horses particularly need ridin'?" Paul asked Casey.

"Well, that little bay over there is just a two-year-old. His name is Lousecake. Guess he's never had a saddle on 'im.'"

"It's about time he got started." Paul looked him over. Lousecake was small and stubby, but had personality. He had the bushy black mane and tail so often found on Indian ponies. In spite of his small size he was well developed for a two-year-old.

With a 'we'd-just-as-well-have-this-out-now' look on his face, Paul picked up a halter and started for the colt. Lousecake made two circuits of the corral at a fast trot, then stopped in a corner and let Paul halter him. The saddle blanket didn't spook him, nor did the saddle and bridle which were cautiously put in place.

Paul led Lousecake around the corral in his new outfit, and the horse offered no objections. I took up the cinch a couple of notches and he still didn't spook. Paul put a foot in the stirrup, then a little weight. The youngster was not too happy but offered no trouble, so Paul said, "Here goes, folks," and swung into the saddle.

Lousecake looked for a minute like he was going to explode, but he didn't, and Paul nudged him around the corral without anything serious happening. Dismounting slowly, carefully, he announced, "I'll ride him home."

Just for the sake of good health he fashioned a hackamore around the horse's nose for an emergency brake then remounted and pushed the other horses out of the corral and down the road.

"I'll probably bed down at the Seven V Four tonight and see you about noon tomorrow. This little guy is soft and I don't want to ride him too hard."

Paul and the horses were on their way, his bedroll lashed to an old packhorse. I loaded the saddles in the trailer and returned to the ranch.

Paul arrived in the early afternoon of the next day, still riding Lousecake. Lucy and I saw them coming and went out to greet them.

"How's that little guy doing?" I asked.

"Okay. Didn't offer any trouble at all, and I've taught him to neck rein pretty good. Look at this." He put the horse through two figure eights and he handled well, considering the short training period.

"He's cute," said Lucy. "What's his name?"

"Lousecake."

"Lousecake!" she exclaimed.

"Yep. Lousecake."

"Now you look, boys. I don't mind this horse business, but we're not having any old crowbaits around called Lousecake. You'll have to change that."

"What do you want to call him?"

"Call him Cactus. He looks like a desert rat anyway, and Cactus will be as good a name as any. He's kind of a nice little guy, isn't he?"

Paul allowed as how he would make a good horse. "He's plumb gentle and quick as a cat. He'll be all right if we can grow him up."

It took a few days to build a corral, put in a water tank, haul hay, buy shoes, ferrier's tools, and the thousand and one things that go with keeping a stable. We had to build a shelter for the saddles, stock the standard remedies and put up highway signs announcing that we had horses for rent.

All the horses had to be ridden and sized up. Cactus would be fine for guests as soon as he had had gentling and more training. Half a dozen of the other horses showed themselves to be foolproof for guest riding. The pinto, Navajo, was more spirited, not easy to mount, and more flashy than useful. Snip was strictly for experienced riders, and keep clear of those heels because he'll let fly with them on any excuse. Lady, the mousey mare, was a devil. She would take a rider alongside a tree, then fall into it to ditch her burden. Try as we might, we couldn't break her of this vicious habit. Paul and I rode her frequently in a vain attempt to get some sense through her thick skull, but she was hopeless as a guest horse so we finally gave up. Her owner came to ride her one day and Lady threw him higher than a kite, breaking his wrist. I don't recall any condolences. We sent Lady home with her owner.

We were proud of our new corral and our horses which were a welcome though expensive addition to our growing family. We were poor but happy, confident that visitors soon would arrive to help us pay the bills.

Lucy was to have the thrill of checking in our first guests.

19

Guests and Horses. It's a Guest Ranch Now.

"I DID IT!" Lucy wore a broad smile as she greeted me on my return from town one afternoon. "I rented a cottage for the whole winter, and to the swellest people. You'll like them. And they think our ranch is great."

This confirmation of our feelings about the ranch was even more important than the rental. Parents love people who love their baby.

"Their names are Bill and Pat Storms," she continued, "and they came from Newport, Washington. Bill spent 23 years in China and was captured there by the Japanese! They know some of the people we met in China. They said this is just what they were looking for. They're in town now, buying groceries."

Her enthusiasm was explosive and it caught me broadside, too. When I saw the first name on our brand new register, my elation matched Lucy's.

Within the hour the Storms returned from their shopping tour of Mesa and their huge boxes of groceries were mute evidence of intent to stay a long time.

Bill and Pat were all Lucy had said, and more. They settled down as part of the family. Together we enjoyed morning coffee on the broad porch which was common to our quarters and theirs. Together we hiked and discovered new things in the desert. Bill and I surveyed our land with the aid of his compass and our long legs, which were equal to metering distance almost exactly a yard at a step. We explored Hieroglyphic Canyon, and Bill and Pat hiked to the highest point of the Superstitions. They laid out a trail to the Hieroglyphics, marking the route with sheets of toilet paper stuck on cactus every few yards. We enjoyed evening visits together and now and then a convivial cocktail at sundown.

Within a short time more parties of guests arrived and our little cottages were filled with pleasant, friendly folks who shared our love of the beauty and tranquility of the desert. Enough money was coming in that we no longer were dipping into our small reserve. We were actually depositing money in the bank! Not much, but the first dribble held encouragement and the assurance that more would follow until ultimately we'd have a secure living.

Mr. and Mrs. Hoffman, an elderly couple from Minnesota occupied the nearest cottage. Mr. and Mrs. Riley, and son Del, took the second cottage.

Mr. and Mrs. Hunchis, their two-year-old daughter Katy and companion Greta arrived from Mason City, Iowa, in a huge maroon Cadillac. We had only a one-room cottage available, but I did not seriously think it would be acceptable to a party of four accustomed to traveling in a Cadillac. They wanted to see it anyway, so I took them to the cottage.

"This is swell," said Fred Hunchis. "If you've got a cot, we'll get along fine. The double bed will hold two of us and I'll sleep on the bunk on the porch."

Fred was a huge man and just as friendly as he was large. His wife, Babe, was a beautiful woman of middle age deeply devoted to her little daughter and family. Gretta Holcomb was a companion and friend to the family. She loved them all and was eager not to miss the slightest detail of the desert and all the activities of the ranch.

Our ranch is simply a big country home where all the visitors are a part of the family. A thoroughly objectionable guest has never come our way. Perhaps it is only good luck, but I like to think the desert has a way of shunning such characters, of becoming unattractive to them.

Fred Hunchis was a stockman accustomed to the out-of-doors. Accordingly, he arose early in the morning and always was the first to make the trek to the men's "convenience." Then it was his custom to return to his cottage, take his coffee pot and cup to the front porch, watch the rest of the ranch gradually come alive, rub its eyes and make the uphill pull to the outhouse. An idea was forming in his fertile brain. For three mornings he let it grow, and on the afternoon of the third day he came to Lucy.

"Tomorrow morning I want you to get up early and put on an extra pot of coffee. You're going to have company for breakfast. Make lots of coffee and have it out on the porch."

The next morning Fred laid in wait, caught each guest as he or she emerged from the johnny, and directed them to our front porch for coffee. Bill Storms was the first to arrive, garbed in his broad Stetson, a silk dressing gown, striped pajamas, and cowboy boots. Fred's next victim was his own wife, Babe, in dressing

gown, silk slippers, and hair tied in curlers. Herb was the rugged type. All he had on was pajama pants and slippers. Mr. Hoffman showed up in his Minnesota fedora, pajamas, topcoat and dress shoes. Esther Riley had slipped into a dress and was the only one who actually looked like she had meant to go to a party. The rest were in their favorite bathrobes, one even sporting a nightpot which he had hoped surreptitiously to keep from the public eye.

One by one they gathered, and each arrival brought new laughs from the growing circle on our front porch. When the last guest had arrived Fred lined us up in the sun for pictures, nightpot and all.

When the shock had passed we settled down to coffee, cakes, eggs and bacon which Lucy miraculously brought in volume from our little wood-burning stove.

Every day half a dozen or more carloads of visitors came to the ranch. Some were prospects, others were just curious. All seemed interested in our project.

In mid-November we were elated when Mr. and Mrs. Prentice from Hartford, Connecticut, returned. They were the folks who had visited us the first day we started digging for the floor of our house, and had wondered how in the world we'd ever attract guests clear up here in the desert.

"My God, King," said Prentice as we shook hands. "You've been working. When we were here last February there wasn't anything but your trailer. Now you've got four buildings. They look good, too. We've been talking about you ever since we first met."

"We've thought about you too," I replied truthfully. "You said you might come back and we always hoped you would. You and your wife look like folks who'd suit this country."

"The wife and I thought we'd come back and stay with you if you'd have us. Can we rent a cabin for a couple of weeks?"

"I'm sorry, but we're full."

"Full? My God, King, I didn't think you'd ever be full! You mean you got guests in all your places?"

"Yes," I said. "There are only four units, but they're all occupied. Mr. and Mrs. Hunchis have to return to Iowa next Wednesday. Why don't you locate along the highway until then and then come take their cottage?"

He looked at his wife. "Let's do it," she said. "I still don't know what all these people are doing clear out here in the desert, but I'd like to find out. We'll be back on Wednesday."

Lucy handed them a book about desert birds and plants. "You take these, Mrs. Prentice. You can read up so when you come back you'll know all about these things."

We sent them off with the book and they returned the following Wednesday to take the cottage vacated by the Hunchis family who had been such fine guests and good friends that everyone on the ranch hated to see them leave.

Mrs. Prentice hopped out of the car like a woman twenty years younger than when we first met her.

"I've been having more fun. Every day I've taken a walk in the desert and I've been finding everything your book tells about. I've seen four different kinds of lizards, quail, rabbits, a fox, desert wrens, Gila woodpeckers, and two street walkers."

My ears pricked up. "Two street walkers?"

"Sure, those things that run fast and have a long tail."

"Oh, you mean road runners!"

"That's what I mean, road runners." Mrs. Prentice blushed. "What was I thinking of anyway?"

We all laughed as I showed them to their cottage.

One night our guests were on the front porch and Paul was holding forth. He was a fair hand at mixing truth and fiction and producing a story not too easy to believe, nor too implausible. This one was a true story about a dead man whose skull he had found in the Superstitions. The group sat in rapt silence. Mrs. Prentice was on the front row, taking in Paul's every word.

"The Sheriff come up here on Sunday morning," Paul said, "and brought a couple of fellers with him. These fellers were dude prospectors and they'd found part of old man Cravey's body in one of those canyons. But they'd got half lost on the way out of the mountains and didn't know how to tell the Sheriff where the body was. So he brought them to us and wanted horses and a guide to get what was left of the old man. So I saddles up some horses and took 'em back into the mountains."

"Who was Cravey?" Mrs. Prentice asked.

"Well, Cravey was an old guy from Phoenix who was a little loco," Paul replied. "He claimed he'd had a vision in the night and had seen a sump — a sump's a canyon closed on both ends — the bottom of it was covered with gold. Shovels full of gold."

Paul continued with the story as the guests settled back and silently begged for more.

"Cravey was outfitted with enough rope to let himself down to the bottom of the canyon where the gold was. He was gimpy in one arm and one leg, but didn't pay it any mind. When he'd got his grub and bedroll together he hired a helicopter to take him into the mountains, and gave the pilot instructions to come back for him in ten days."

The pilot returned, according to Paul, but Cravey failed to appear. His camp was still supplied with unused provisions and water. A fire had been built but the place had been occupied only a short time. The pilot hovered over the area but couldn't locate Cravey, so he returned to Phoenix and reported it to the Sheriff.

The Sheriff did what he could to locate Cravey, but it was a hopeless task without leads. The summer heat was at its height, water was scarce in the mountains and men who knew the country and climate did not lightly undertake hunting lost prospectors.

"By fall Cravey's name had long since passed from the front pages of the newspapers," Paul continued, "and nobody would ever have found him if these two dudes hadn't gone prospecting and wandered into one of the most dangerous canyons in the mountains. The walls were steep and covered with brush that hid the loose, rolling rocks. It was hard to get into and double hard to get out of. But there in the bottom, in the choking catclaw underbrush, these men found what was left of a human form. The denim pants were still okay and they found a wallet belonging to old Cravey in the hip pocket. They couldn't find the boots, feet or the head, and the parts they did find had been scattered by animals.

"They tore right back to tell the Sheriff, so he came to the ranch for a guide and horses."

"Oooooh!" exclaimed Mrs. Prentice when Paul had finished. "Did you get to the body, Paul?"

"Sure, I found it. Them bones was pretty well scattered. The coyotes had been achewin' on 'em and they was pretty well beat up, but we found 'em — all but the head and feet."

"No head? No feet? For heaven's sakes, how did he get into the canyon without any feet?"

"He walked in, I guess. But you see, lady, the chances are the first night he was a layin' there dead, a pack of coyotes found him and started fightin' over the meat."

By now the women in the audience were sucking air between their teeth.

"One old coyote figures the head's a good deal for him, so he tears it loose and lights off across the warsh where he could gnaw on it all alone. That's just where I finally found it, right across the warsh in a little blowout in the rocks. So I put the skull under my arm…"

"You put the skull under your arm?"

"Sure, lady. Had to carry it back to the pack horse. We picked up all the other bones we could find, threw 'em into the panniers, carried 'em out of the mountains and give 'em to the Coroner. The Coroner in Pinal County is a big, fat old lady who couldn't ride a horse nowhere."

"Didn't you ever find the man's feet, Paul?" asked Bill Storm.

"Nope. I don't know what ever happened to 'em. Some folks around here say he'd had a riot with his family, had taken all his money out of the bank — three to four thousand — and sewed it in the lining of his boot. I heard that after we was in there. I didn't have time to look for 'em a helluvamuch because the Sheriff was in a hurry to get home."

"Mercy, think of that! Finding a dead man." Mrs. Prentice was properly impressed by Paul's true story.

"Shucks, lady, we find one every once in a while. We got one buried right by the corner post of the corral."

"A dead man buried by the corner post of the corral?" gasped Mrs. Prentice, not realizing that a deadman was the name for a big rock to which a guy wire is fastened.

"Sure, lady, a deadman."

"Paul, I don't believe it. You're not telling the truth. Imagine, a dead man buried right here on this ranch."

"It's just as true as God made little wigglin' rattlesnakes. I'll dig it up for you to prove it, but I ain't agoin' to do all that diggin' for nothin'."

"I tell you what I'll do, Paul." Mrs. Prentice's blood pressure stood at about 220. "You dig him up and if there's a dead man

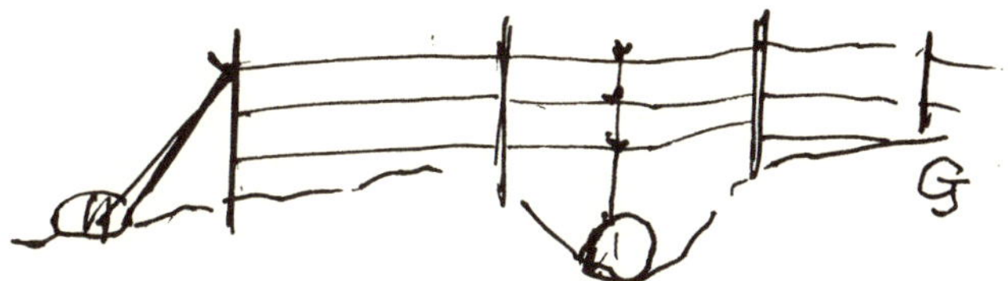

there I'll give you $5.00. If there isn't, you gotta give me a free horseback ride. Come on, let's start digging."

"You mean dig up a deadman on a pitch-dark night?" Paul was bent on making this a real adventure for Mrs. Prentice, something she could lose sleep over. "I wouldn't do it for $500. But I'll do it in the morning if you want. I can use that five bucks."

"Now all you people heard that, didn't you?" Mrs. Prentice polled the crowd. "Okay, now, we'll all meet at the corral at 7:00 in the morning."

"Okay, Ma'am," said Paul as he walked off the front porch toward the corral. "7:00, I'll have the horses fed."

The whole crowd appeared at 7:00 a.m. They weren't all dressed for the day, but they all were there when Paul first swung the pick over his shoulder. In five minutes he'd rolled the big rock, with the barbed wire wrapped around its belly, at Mrs. Prentice' feet.

"That's no dead man," yelled Mrs. Prentice.

"It shore is, Ma'am," smiled Paul. "You just go look in the dictionary up at the house and then get yourself into a long trot down here to the corral with that five bucks of mine."

Mr. Prentice spent the rest of his visit telling every new arrival about how that bow-legged cowboy had educated his wife for five bucks. She blushed every time he told the story, and Paul's face showed a knowing smirk at every reference to how he'd "done in the dude."

In March of that first season we gathered a little money and enough credit to install butane gas and an automatic electric light plant. Lucy and I were proud of our new conveniences. Although it was a breach of the frontier way of life, we thought our guests would be grateful for the added amenities of electric lights, gas stoves, and heaters.

But guests are unpredictable. "Do I have to give up my cute little wood stove? I just love it, and it reminds me so much of when I was a youngster," said Mrs. Riley.

"I sure do like my oil lamp," said Mrs. Hoffman. "It sheds such soft, gentle light — just like we used to have on the farm. I suppose you have to put in electricity to please some folks, but August and I are happy with our lamp," she said, somewhat grudgingly.

Over the succeeding five years we modernized everything, but sometimes wonder whether it was not more fun in the beginning. The wood-burning cook stoves were warm and friendly. They provided a novel change from city habits and folks liked them. The kerosene lamps' soft, restful light was more than adequate for ranch life. The evenings were quiet and everyone retired early, the better to enjoy the refreshing desert mornings. The ice boxes were not handy, for ice had to be hauled thirty miles from Mesa. It was a messy business, but they were a means to an end and acceptable.

The lack of a modern water system was the real inconvenience. We were still experiencing the shortages brought on by the war, iron pipe being the scarcest commodity of all for those first few years. We still had to use barrels on the back of each cottage, hauling water to them each morning in a trailer. Water was heated on the stove. The supply was limited to fifty gallons per cottage on any one day, for that was the capacity of the barrels and we could haul only once a day.

For some reason, flush toilets were impossible. Outhouses bring to former country folks nostalgic memories of youth and all the comical events which centered around the farm yard in days gone by. But to modern city dwellers they bear mysteries, and to a considerable degree, misgivings. We had to rationalize our plumbing shortcomings by recalling that only a few years ago nearly everyone in Arizona was in the same fix, but they all lived in health and happiness, and led more or less normal lives. For the people accustomed to nothing but tiled baths, our rustic "convenience" was anything but.

Saturday night baths here had to be in the old country style. Many of our guests of the first season recalled how, when they were kids, their mothers heated water in a big tub atop the kitchen stove on Saturday night and called them, one by one, into the kitchen to be scrubbed down vigorously while standing in a smaller tub on the floor. They recalled the children's weekly protests and the rush to get the whole family bathed and dressed for their visit to town.

City-raised folks just didn't know how, so had to be instructed in great detail. It was surprising how little complaint there was and they seemed to enjoy it and glean satisfaction from finding they were not completely dependent upon modern gadgets. They gained a better understanding of the lot of pioneers and the early West and were even a little proud to know they could hold their own with those rugged old-timers.

Now that the ranch is modernized, those early inconveniences are but food for reminiscing.

20

"What Can You Do for Two Maiden Ladies?"

DURING THE FOUR MONTHS THEY WERE OUR GUESTS, a very pleasant friendship had arisen between Bill and Pat Storms and Lucy and me. The Storms were the sort of folks who wanted, like us, to establish a winter home on the ranch. It seemed like a wonderful idea to have them for permanent neighbors. Bill and Pat were energetic hikers and had covered every inch of our property, so they knew exactly where they would like to build, and it was not long before we had arranged it.

This was a new development and a wonderful one. What could be nicer, we thought, than to have here and there on the ranch some attractive winter homes where good friends would live — folks we would like to have walk into our own home now and then for some sociability? The money which came to us in this manner we could put right back into the development of the ranch.

Upon completion of their plans for building the following fall, Bill and Pat left for their home in the north the first of April.

The sale of a few parcels of land was a stroke of good fortune totally unanticipated. We didn't realize at the time we would be solving the winter home problems of so many splendid families, and would acquire such fine neighbors and fast friends. That spring we were grateful for the nice boost over another financial hump. Thus began our snug little ranch community which, through the years, has grown most pleasantly.

We wrote Father and Mother about our good fortune, and they were both pleased and impressed. They had developed a better understanding of what we were doing and this added proof that other people wanted to live in our desert encouraged them to believe our scheme was not completely insane. We lacked some things they still thought very important, but all in all their views had gone through an almost complete reversal.

At last Father was persuaded to retire. He could have worked several years longer, thus increasing his income upon retirement, but we argued that if they gambled a few more years' work against the continuance of good health, they might lose. They finally agreed.

They arrived in the spring. Mother went over everything and sympathetically wept about all the hard work we had done. It hadn't seemed to us like a particularly tough life, but to her it was a sacrificial labor of love. Lucy for Julian, Julian for Lucy — an epic of devotion.

They liked Paul and Paul liked them. He called them "Mother and Father King," to their delight. Mother undertook his mending along with ours. A cowboy's sewing is a fearful and astonishing thing, so there was plenty of scope for Mother's talents.

The folks had spent many months laying out the plans for their home. When they were ready I helped them hire a couple of men and got them started with the work. I shall always regret that when Mother and Father arrived I was so busy with guests, visitors and daily chores that I couldn't be of more help on their new home. Lucy and I would have enjoyed building it ourselves, and with Father's help — or perhaps I should say with us helping Father — we'd have done it well and quickly. The best I could do was give some supervision and instruction to the men he hired.

Mother had mixed feelings about the size of her house. She wanted it large enough for comfort but small enough to keep housework to a minimum. It kept all the men guessing, trying to arrive at his happy medium. I think we might have done it if the happy medium had stayed in the same place.

She watched the progress of pouring the concrete floor with great interest but threw everything into a tizzy when, right in the middle of the job, she exclaimed, "My goodness, Bruce, this house isn't going to be half big enough!"

Father made his way out of that one as best he could. I stayed clear, leaving it to Father to convince her it really would be exactly the size she had decided upon.

A couple of weeks later, when the rock walls were about three feet high, she walked to the center of the floor and looked around, grave disturbance clearly showing in her eyes.

"My goodness, Bruce," she said, "this is going to be an enormous house for me to keep clean!"

I took off and the workers snickered at Father's predicament. She was back in good spirits in a few minutes and busy visualizing where she was going to place each piece of furniture. This occupation made her days busy ones and she had everything planned long before the roof was on the house.

During our pleasant evenings together we discussed many things. One thing, inexplicable to us, was the mail which came to us from all over the country from folks we'd never heard of and wondered how they had heard of us. We had been fortunate in receiving some publicity during our first season and always thought this might have been responsible.

A schoolgirl in Connecticut wrote, "Dear Mr. King. We are studying geography in our class in school, and I've been chosen to find out all about Apache Indians. Since your address is Apache Junction, Arizona, I thought you would know all about

Apaches. Will you please write me all about them, send me books and tell me where I can get more information."

Every week in the spring we received appeals for employment, of which the following was representative:

"Dear Sir: We have two lovely daughters, ages sixteen and eighteen, who have their hearts set on working at a western ranch during their summer vacations. Both are intelligent, attractive, and lead their respective classes in school. The younger, Ann, is a physical education student, so we are confident she would be wonderful around horses. She also has a splendid voice and could entertain your guests by singing in the evenings. Her sister, Joan, is very good at home economics so I'm sure she will be of great help to you in serving and preparing food for your guests. She also reads western novels avidly and would be right at home in Arizona. Of course, both are young and should have some protection from romantic cowboys. I'd have to ask that you give your word in this regard."

A travel agent in New York corresponded with us at intervals about prospective guests. He asked if we would permit a guest to bring his dog, and in support of his belief in our mutual love for animals, added: "I know how you get attached to animals. As a matter of fact my cat, which I got in Arizona two years ago, has just about broken up my marriage. My wife hates cats, she hates the West, in fact she hates about everything I love. She made life so miserable for all of us I had to take the cat out of the house and I keep him in my office (he is smiling at me now — KNOWS I am writing about him) and he knows, I'LL NEVER PART WITH HIM. Please advise pronto about the above prospective guest and if you can, advise me on what I should do. It looks as if my married life is gone. I'd appreciate it."

A lady in New Jersey, with whom I carried on a considerable correspondence, finally asked if there would be a chaise lounge in her "apartment!" That correspondence ended abruptly.

One day I opened my mail and quite seriously read the following inquiry to Lucy:

"Dear Mr. King. Will you please let me know what you can do for two traveling maiden ladies?"

Lucy almost burst. "Just tell them, 'Very little.'"

In due course Mother and Father's house was done, a huge van arrived from Washington and with the help of all hands, they soon were moved in. The neighbors and guests suggested a house-warming. It was an idea dear to Mother's hospitable heart so one was arranged promptly.

All the guests and neighbors came, as did Paul. He was dressed in his western best. His face was polished, his hair combed and boots shined. We were proud of him.

During the evening Father was called upon for a speech. He had a penchant for becoming president or chairman of any group he joined, for he is affable, the members all know he'll do all the work, and he knows how most any kind of organization ought to operate. This led to his being a capable speech maker. One of his chief interests had been the church, and he held almost every office in it at one time or another. He and Mother faithfully conduct themselves as the good Methodists they are. That's why I was astonished at Father's speech. It wasn't a speech, it was a story:

"Did you ever hear the one about the horse trader who was not good with figures?" No one said they had, so he continued. "Well, two men were engaged in a horse trade. The buyer was very poor at arithmetic and the seller knew it, so the seller decided to fool his friend with a proposition he couldn't understand. He said, 'I'll sell you this horse for $100, take off 10 percent.' The buyer didn't understand the offer and didn't want to admit his lack of knowledge so he told his friend he would have an answer in the morning.

"That evening he went to the restaurant for dinner and decided he'd try his problem on the waitress. When she came to his table he asked her, 'If I said I'd give you $100.00, take off 10 percent, what would you take off?'

"Hell, Mister, for that kind of money I'd take off everything but my earrings."

That kind of story from my father almost broke up the party. The evening ended with "For he's a jolly good fellow…"

Rarely did we have a ranch party that someone did not ask him to repeat the "story about 10 percent off." He fulfilled their wishes more times than suited Mother, who never realized her "Bruce, for heaven's sake don't tell that awful story again," just nudged him into accepting the challenge.

21

Mother's Adopted Son

AT THE TIME OF THE HOUSEWARMING we had two British ladies as ranch guests. Outwardly, at least, they acted as though they shouldn't unbend and laugh at Father's story but they had difficulty suppressing their laughter in the presence of the other roaring guests.

They were Mrs. Judith Bothwell-Sandringham and Miss Madeleine Springbottom, according to the register, and they resided in Quebec, Canada. Until they invited us to call them by their first names, Judith and Madeleine, we had an awful time. Everyone on the ranch was talking about these interesting newcomers, but hardly knew how to address them.

Mrs. Prentice finally settled the matter. She struggled through "Bothingham-Sandringwell," "Wellingham-Sandybottom," and several other combinations before deciding to shorten it to "B-S" and letting it go at that. The idea caught on with everyone.

When they arrived, Judith had said, "Miss Springbottom and I should like to spend a couple of weeks with you if you can accommodate us. We shall require two cottages with private bawth."

I swallowed twice before explaining about our private "bawth" arrangement, and was amazed when they accepted what we had. It was at the end of the season and, luckily, two cottages were available, so they moved in.

B-S was a handsome tall blonde woman in her late forties. In her younger days she had been a dramatic actress, she said, and had headlined performances all over the world. Her husband had to remain in Quebec because of business, so she had acquired Madeleine as a traveling companion-maid, in sort of a friend-of-the-family way.

Madeleine had been a charming acquaintance for many years. She had not married and circumstances had forced her to live modestly, but she was a cultured woman devoted to drawma and that is how they first met.

Judith's husband was high on Canada's financial and social rosters, and Judith was a little embarrassed that the Canadian government's economic restrictions of that time did not allow her to carry as much cash to the United States as would enable her to live in her accustomed style. I think that was the real reason she was at Kings Ranch.

I've always regretted that Judith couldn't be "ranch-broke" for she was as attractive and interesting a person as I have ever met. When she turned on the charm she captivated everyone in range and her broad traveling experience made her an engaging conversationalist. But she could not get away from her stage acting, high heels, flowing black silk dressing gowns and high society manners. Both were lovely ladies but fit a ranch about as well as Quick would have fit Buckingham Palace.

Judith had a Pekingese dog and Madeleine owned a black poodle, both a little fancy for Blackie's taste, but he tolerated them as long as neither trespassed on his front porch. When either guest dog passed the house with his mistress, Blackie sat on the edge of his porch and growled a warning against intrusion. Judith and Madeleine always kept their dogs on leashes, lest they wander into the cactus or become a meal for a passing coyote.

The two guests, Lucy, and I were visiting on our front porch one afternoon. By being stern, Lucy had made Blackie lie quietly under a bunk. Judith and Madeleine clutched their leashes tightly and all was peace and quiet when Tony, the cowboy, rode up to the house.

"Who is that savage looking person?" whispered B-S.

"He's a Yaqui cowboy who rides for our neighbors, the Barkleys," I explained.

"What is a Yaqui?"

"A Yaqui is half-Mexican, half-Indian."

B-S drew her robes around her more tightly.

"What you doing, Tony?" I called.

"Ridin' the fence, Meester King. You got beer, Meester King? Tony thirsty."

I got Tony a cold beer. Tony never carried water and usually was out of tobacco, so I was surprised when he fished the makings out of his shirt pocket and rolled a smoke. His horse was ground tied by the front step and Tony sat down near the reins to enjoy his beer and cigarette.

"How's the gall bladder, Tony?"

"Oh she just the same. She just lie still like that rock an' do nuthin'. Mees Barkley, he gall bladder still jump around like loco horse, Meester King. Mees Barkley feel bad too when he gall bladder go like that." Tony finished his beer and stomped out his cigarette. Reaching for his reins, he said, "Thank you Mees and Meester King. Now I go ride fence some more."

B-S was bewildered. When Tony was out of ear shot she said, "I must say I am confused about this person who rides on a fence."

As I gathered my thoughts for an explanation I offered Judith a cigarette. She accepted and in doing so, released her hold on the Pekingese's leash.

All Hell broke loose. The Peke lunged for Blackie, the poodle lunged for the Peke, the two women popped out of their chairs screaming, and everyone started kicking, swinging and shouting. I finally reached into the middle of the dog fight and grabbed Blackie. I lifted him clear of the other dogs, and in so doing caught the Peke with a solid boot kick on the hind quarters. In the melee someone nicked B-S's shins.

"Madeleine, you silly awss, you kicked me," shrieked B-S.

"Judith darling, I certainly did not."

"Madeleine, precious, I am not telling an untruth. You kicked me and I shall welcome your apology at any time."

She strode off the stage in her most haughty rage. Madeleine pursued with proper apologies and by evening the wound seemed healed.

A day later Mrs. Bothwell-Sandringham was shocked to receive a telegram saying her 97-year-old mother had passed away. She was grief stricken. We helped her all we could and at her suggestion, I drove her to Phoenix and arranged passage on the first plane going east. She said she would return as soon as affairs at home were in order, that she would wire Madeleine of her arrival, so she could be met at the airport.

Our arrangement for receiving telegrams was undependable. The telegraph company had instructions to telephone messages to the postmaster at Apache Junction, then to mail the telegram to this address. The next person coming to the ranch would bring the mail, but sometimes a day or two would elapse before anyone made the trip. Thus, Judith's wire saying she would arrive at Phoenix airport at 10:00 a.m. got caught in a double foul-up.

The company failed to telephone the message and when Father picked up the mail the morning of Judith's arrival he considered the telegram of such importance that he put it in a special pocket — and promptly forgot about it. In late afternoon he chanced to change his clothes and found the wire.

"Oh my gosh," he said to Mother and streaked to Madelaine's cottage with the news that Judith should have arrived at the Phoenix airport hours ago.

"Mercy, this *is* a bloody mess," Madeleine said, as she hurriedly prepared for the trip to Phoenix to rescue Judith. Father and I were cowards. Neither of us offered to go along.

Judith had arrived on schedule. Her seven-hour wait in the public waiting room, a place well below her station, our negligence, and her grief had resulted in a horrible state of affairs by the time Madeleine came to the rescue. It was evening when they got back to the ranch so they went straight to their respective cottages.

Mother considered the situation a personal burden. Father had been the cause of all the trouble and Mother was in deep sympathy with Judith, in her grief. So early next morning she made a very proper call.

No one had ever had sweeter, kindlier intentions than Mother, but there have been times when she has succeeded only in gumming things up.

Judith was weeping as Mother entered. In her best motherly manner she tried to comfort Judith by saying how wonderful it was that her Mother had lived such a full 97 years, and since the doctors said she could not possibly have recovered, it had been a blessing that she had been taken on to her reward quickly, without long suffering.

When Mother later told us about it we thought it was a particularly fitting and comforting approach, but Judith had almost gone into convulsions, saying Mother was cruel to suggest that it was a blessing that her mother had passed on. My Mother was crushed. She apologized, wept with Judith, and they apparently went on together at such length that the subject was finally exhausted. They recovered their composure and entered into a fairly normal conversation, except that Judith could not forget Mother's unintentionally belittling her grief.

The conversation somehow reverted to me, giving Judith the opportunity she needed to turn the tables.

"I think Julian is a splendid young man," she said to Mother, who beamed. "Isn't it remarkable that he fits into your life so beautifully when he is an adopted son?"

"Adopted son! Adopted son!" Nothing could have dealt Mother a more telling blow. "He's my own flesh and blood. My own FLESH AND BLOOD!" she cried tearfully, as she slammed the door and ran to our house in worse state than Judith ever had been.

"Some people think I can't do *anything*," she wept.

That afternoon Madeleine loaded Judith and her belongings in her car and they came to our door. Lucy met them.

"I'm sorry, but I think we must leave," Judith said.

"Yes, I think perhaps it is just as well," Lucy agreed, and our suffering British friends departed the desert.

22

I Try to Reform a Liar

AMONG OUR VISITORS IN THE SPRING was a young man of twenty-two who introduced himself as "California Joe" Dawton, late of the United States navy, the rodeo circuits, Hollywood, Texas, Mexico, and anyplace else one might mention. He addressed everyone as "Podna," and laid claim to a fame almost beyond belief, even in itinerant cowboys.

Joe was dressed in customary western garb of well-faded Levi's, striped shirt with pearl snaps, boots and a Stetson. The broad brimmed hat, however, was cocked at the jaunty Hollywood angle instead of flat, close-to-the-eyebrows manner usual to an Arizona range cowboy. He claimed to be a wrangler, builder, plumber, actor, mechanic and affable all around guy who would be great at entertaining guests and increasing our business with his cleverness. He liked the country, wanted to find the Lost Dutchman Gold Mine, and could do us a lot of favors in the meantime, if we only would put him on the payroll. He looked as though he'd like to call me "Bud."

I told him I had a man and needed another about like a horse needs three ears.

"Well, Podna, I'm sorry you can't see your way clear to use me right now. I'd do you a heap of good besides helpin' ya'." And with that he left.

About a month later Lucy noticed two figures walking up the road.

When they got close enough for recognition she called to me, "Good Lord! I wish you'd see who's coming up the road." It was California Joe and a woman. Each was carrying a heavy back pack and they were coming right to the house.

"Mr. King, I'd like to have you meet my wife, Lily. Her old man is a big shot in Michigan. They'd do you a lot of good — know a lot of rich people you could get to come to your ranch." Joe and Lily slipped the packs off their backs. "Me and Lily hiked up here about fifteen miles, but we're good for another fifteen today. We're both a rarin' to go. Not even thirsty."

This must be leading to something.

"Me and Lily sure like the country, Podna, and I'd like your permission to spread our bedrolls down by the wash and stay a while. It's kinda in between seasons in my regular business, so I'll work for ya to pay for stayin'."

It was nearing the end of the guest season and we were preparing to build three new cottages during the summer. I could use another strong back with the heavy work in the beginning, and this boy seemed to have it. If he wasn't any good we could let him go. If I didn't pay I couldn't fire him, so I made him an offer.

"I won't let you work for nothing," I told him, "but I'll pay you a weekly wage if you'll do a good job. If you don't, I'll tell you to move on."

"Oh, I'll work good. You needn't worry about Lily and me, Podna. We'll take care of ourselves and not bother you a bit. If you'll give me the rest of the day to make camp, build us a fireplace and rustle some wood I'll go to work early in the morning."

It was sort of a cockeyed deal, but why not? It could be ended as quickly as it had begun.

Paul was still the head wrangler, so Joe was told not to waste time around the corral. He and Lily could ride after work if Paul gave his permission and it did not infringe upon the guests' riding. Above all, he and Lily were not to interfere with the guests in any way, and were to be polite to them at all times. This boy was a new hand and could stand a little trimming down.

The next morning two young men hired us to pack their supplies and equipment into the Superstitions. They had located a claim in Needle Canyon and would have four or five hundred pounds to be packed in, come next Thursday. They showed us the spot on the map where their camp lay and gave Paul a detailed description of the location. We asked them to have their gear at the ranch the day prior to the trip.

I told Paul to handle the pack because I was busy with guests and preparations for building, and added he could take Joe along if he thought he needed help. The two boys did not see eye to eye on everything. In fact Paul thought Joe was a Hollywood drugstore cowboy, so I was not surprised when Paul insisted that he needed no help.

Paul said, "What we need for this packing is some burros. I know where there are three good ones that we can get for not a helluvamuch. They'd get along on the desert without us feeding them and it'd save the horses."

He had half a dozen other arguments in favor of burros, so I consented. Lucy and I are suckers for animals and three burros would add to our growing menagerie.

I told the boys to hitch up the horse trailer and go get the burros. Lucy wanted to do some shopping in town, so she went along. Late that afternoon the Ford appeared on the road, drawing the horse trailer and its burden. But I could see only two burro heads.

"Where's the third burro? I thought you said you could get all three in one trip?" I asked Lucy and Paul.

"Gabriel's in the bottom of the trailer."

Sure enough, "Gabriel" got in and laid down and all the King's men and women couldn't budge him. Diablo's front hooves bore into Gabriel's neck, and Jennifer's feet were gouging Gabriel's hind quarters, but Gabriel still seemed to think he had the best of the deal because he was still lying down.

"Who named that jackass 'Gabriel?"

"I did," said Lucy. "You ought to hear him blow his horn."

The reasons for Diablo's name became apparent as soon as we tried to unload the ornery critter. He had the Devil's own ingenuity for causing trouble. He could be ornery at both ends and the middle at the same time. "Jennifer" was an appropriate name for a jennie. She was the only one of the lot that rated a little affection.

Gabriel's neck and hind quarters were cut by the sharp hooves of his traveling companions and Diablo's hide was split straight across the rump by his insistence on pushing back against the tail gate all the way home. But none of these injuries bothered either burro in the slightest. They have no nerves to register pain, I am convinced.

The prospectors showed up on time with their gear, and early the next morning we packed the burros. Paul was certain, he said, where to deliver the equipment. He planned to stay over night and return the next day and, accordingly, threw on his own bedroll and a sack of grub.

I didn't agree with Paul's idea that he could handle the job alone, because the burros were an unknown quantity and he obstinately planned to use a trail he had not been over but was sure would save a lot of time. So I told Joe to pack his blankets and go along. I rode with them a few miles to see that the burros were not entirely useless. The beasts were being a bit stubborn, but the boys were moving steadily, so I turned back to the ranch. As I left I wished them good luck, but should have wished harder.

We watched for them all the following afternoon and evening, but no sign of horses, burros or wranglers. Their failure to show up was a disappointment, but we were not overly surprised. Lily did the only worrying. The evening of the third day an old truck rattled into the yard and dumped Paul and Joe. A strange driver said, "Here's your boys!" and drove off. Both were half starved, scratched, cut and as thoroughly beaten up as a couple of young colts after fighting a snubbing post.

I gave them each a good stiff drink and Lucy started rounding up food. The drink revived their spirits considerably, and they went after the food like shipwrecked sailors. This was their first in a day and a half.

"Well, what happened? And where are the horses and burros?" I asked after deciding they weren't going to offer the information.

"Those damn burros!" said Paul. "If I never see them again it will be too soon. I reckon Joe and I did twice as much packin' as they did. That Jennifer is all right but I'd a shot Diablo if it hadn't been too good treatment for him. And that Gabriel — he didn't do a helluvamuch better."

Paul went on to tell us that Diablo didn't do anything worse than lay back and bust his lead rope about every mile on the way up. "But once we got in the mountains where we couldn't bring him back, he just got tired and laid down. Pack and all. Joe and I took after him with spurs, cactus, rocks, you name it. Joe wrung his tail while I tried to pull him up with my horse, but he wouldn't twitch a muscle. Even lit matches two at a time and held 'em under his tail, but he didn't blink an eye. Didn't dare to build a fire under him with the pack on; we'd of burned up his packs, he was that stubborn."

"Did you chew his ears?"

"I'll be spittin' hide and hair for the next month," answered Joe, puckering his lips to show how you spit out burro hide and hair.

"Where is he now? Still sitting there in the mountains?"

"No, soon's we took his packs off he got right up, and soon's we put 'em back on, he hunkered down again. So there's nothin' to do but leave him with his pack and come back for 'im, and that's what we did. By then it's pretty late and when it got dark we was in Needle Canyon and that's a stinkin' and brushy a place as Hell ever dreamed up. So, Joe and me was stuck with trying to find those guys in Needle Canyon in the middle of the night. About five minutes after dark we lost the trail, and from then on we just stumbled around in the rocks and brush. We fired shots in the air, hollered until we was hoarse, and finally found them dudes about 10:00 that night. We sure was pooped!"

"Next mornin' we had to go back to get Diablo and his pack. That took us all mornin' and part of the afternoon. He wouldn't carry a pack ten feet so we had to use Jennifer.

"Mr. King (Joe occasionally turned formal) I'd'a broke that Diablo's neck if I hadn't a known you wanted him back. He's the no goodest critter I ever seen, an' ornery to boot."

"Okay, you guys delivered your packs yesterday afternoon and had the stock all together. What happened then?"

I was anxious to know where the horses and burros were now.

"Well," Paul said, "By the time we had got everything settled it was too late to go anywheres because we sure didn't want to travel any more at night in that damn canyon. So we hobbled the horses and burros out to feed, and bedded down with them prospectors. Joe, here, had only brought one can of grub and what I'd brought we'd ate the night before, so we didn't have nothin'. Those guys weren't beggin' us to eat up their grub so we just bummed some grounds and had a coupla cups 'a mud and turned in. Next mornin' the horses had got clear out of the country. It was kinda late by the time we tracked 'em down and got everything together, so we decided to take the short way out on the other side of the mountain.

"By this time it was nearly dark and we might have to do something yet tonight, so I asked them where they went and again, where the stock was.

"Rode out to Charley Weeks' place and put the horses and burros in his corral. Charley wasn't there, but he won't mind. Threw 'em a little of Charley's feed. They're all right. We'll get 'em in the mornin'."

The next morning I took Joe and Paul to Charley's in the car. His place was fourteen miles from home by road, and nearly as far afoot, the way you have to trail around the mountain. When we drove up to the corral it didn't take an Indian scout to see that the gate was swinging in the wind and not an animal in sight.

"Guess the wind changed," said Paul.

"Good Lord! What's the wind got to do with the horses?"

"Well, there was a big breeze blowin' from the south that held the gate closed and I guess I didn't lock it."

"*Guess* you didn't lock it? You know damn well you didn't lock it."

"Yea, now that ya mention it, guess that's right."

"You guys get out and start tracking and don't come back 'till you find that stock. We've got work to do and we've already lost three days we shouldn't have because you wouldn't take my advice and stick to the trails you knew."

I'm not fast on catching fire, but I burn fairly hot once the coals are stirred. We left their saddles and bridles at the corral and I watched them start off afoot with catch ropes in their hands.

Late the second day they rode in, driving the burros ahead. The stock had wandered nearly fifteen miles from the corral — probably hadn't been behind that fence an hour. Maybe not half an hour. We had a couple of very quiet cowboys for a week or more, always willing to do whatever needed doing without argument.

Paul and Joe thought the sun rose and set on Lucy. She did many things for them which merited this feeling, and she was always the center of their friendly kidding. They tested her quick wit at every opportunity but never outwitted her. They respected her for getting out and working hard. When she told them to quit leaning on that manure fork and get the corral clean, she got action. They knew very well she meant what she said, that she'd cleaned the corral a time or two herself and knew how the job was done.

Joe hadn't been around long before we realized he was a professional liar without equal in my experience. His brass first became apparent one evening when all of us were sitting on the front porch enjoying each other's company following a hard day's work.

The conversation turned to rattlesnakes, as it often does in the desert. It was late spring and none of us yet had seen one.

"Shucks," said Joe, "these ain't proper rattlers in this country. Texas is where they all are. They really got 'em down in that state. First time I ever seen Texas, Dad was bringin' the family out to California in early spring. There was me and Dad and Mom and my three sises and two young brothers. We stopped in a tourist cabin in a little town out in the hills, and all of us was in the one cabin. We carried bedrolls because it was cheaper if we all got in one cabin. Anyhow, while Mom was gittin' supper we heard a noise down under the floor. It was a wood floor with some room underneath.

"Over in the corner," Joe continued, "there was a little trap door in the floor. Dad found it first and lifted the lid. God, when we looked down in there it was just crawlin' with rattlers. They was big, too. Big around as your arm. Looked like hunnerts of 'em. Now you might not believe this but I swear to God it's true. You ask my Dad today and he'll tell you it's true.

"My old man sent the kids outside for a pole or somethin' to pull 'em out with, and they come back with a rake. You know, just a garden rake like we got down to the corral. Dad started hookin' out snakes and throwin' 'em out the front door, and he hooked and throwed I guess an hour. They just laid out there in a pile — didn't seem to want to crawl away. When he got through there was a pile of snakes as high as my Dad's belly button, and he's purty good size. Now you can believe me or not, but so help me it's true."

"What'd you do then, snap their heads off with your bare hands?" asked Paul, with a smirk on his face.

"Naw, we poured gasoline on 'em and burned 'em up. Never seen a better grease fire in your life. Mom was mad because we didn't skin 'em for meat. It's good."

"Now, Joe," I said, "how many rattlesnakes do you think were under that house?"

"Over three thousand. I counted the rattles after the fire went out. The biggest one," as if the story had to be bigger to clinch it, "was 43 feet long. It started to get away, and we had to kill it."

"Now Joe, look." My credulity was insultingly taxed. "This porch we're sitting on is 42 feet long. Do you mean to sit there and tell me that snake was longer than this porch?"

"Yessir, boss, it was so long that you had to have a bicycle to get from one end to the other when it got moving."

Nobody could top that one, so it broke up the evening's conversation. Joe sulked as our comments about his truthfulness got very salty.

Each day brought more tall tales about things that didn't need stretching at all. Few of the fibs were important except for the fact that he lied when he didn't need to. I puzzled about it. We had not been hurt by his bad habit — or rare talent — but such a persistent liar couldn't be around long without ultimately doing some harm or causing embarrassment. So I called him aside.

"Joe," I said, "I've seen lots of liars but you're the hardest working one I've met yet." To my surprise he took it calmly. "I can't figure out why you do it. You've lied so many times, neither Lucy nor I can trust you."

I had arranged to have his wife present for my little sermon. She sat quietly.

"You're a good enough worker but I can't have a guy around who lies like you do."

On reflection I don't know exactly how I got started preaching, but I was on a roll.

"I've been around a lot more than you have, Joe, and I've known a lot of men. But I never knew a liar to get far. If you'll settle down and watch yourself and stick to the truth we'll get along and you'll go a lot further in this old world."

Was this the voice of experience? I sounded a little sanctimonious to myself, but Joe was sitting tight and was so interested I was encouraged to think I might make a useful human being out of an otherwise warped character.

"Honesty is the greatest thing in the world, Joe, and it is easier to be honest than not. You'll be able to face your friends better if you always tell them the truth. People will trust you and pay you more. Nobody trusts a liar or gives him responsibility."

My unexpected eloquence was about to reach its crest.

"Joe, I want to see you do well, to get along. I'd like to help you right your ways and be successful — someday to run a big cattle spread somewhere. You can do it if you'll just make up your mind, quit lying, and do what I say."

I squared my shoulders and looked him in the eye, amazing myself. "You've got brains, Joe. All you need is to work hard and be honest."

Joe sat quietly, a serious expression on his face.

"Boss, you're right. I've been a liar all my life. I don't know why unless it's because my dad was one too."

"You said it!" his wife chimed in.

"Keep your big mouth shut, sweetheart," Joe said. "I'm serious. I want to do right. I want to work for you. I can see how I could do you wrong by lying. Boss, you've shown me the light. I appreciate your telling me. Never thought about it before, but you're right as they come. Here's my promise. I'll never tell another lie, boss."

He extended his hand. The bargain was sealed with a vigorous shake.

Lily looked amazed but said nothing beyond "Thanks, Mr. King."

I watched them walk down the hill to their camp. Both were serious, perhaps a little repentant, and I was reminded of people walking down a sawdust revival tent aisle.

The next afternoon some friends came from Mesa for horseback riding. The boys and I were right in the middle of pouring concrete for a water reservoir. I couldn't leave the job and I could spare Joe better than Paul, so I told Joe to go saddle horses and take them to the Hieroglyphics. He fairly strutted. It was the first time I had put him in complete charge of a riding party. He bloomed with the responsibility and recognition, and lit off on a good run for the corral. Presently he returned to the house with the horses and with a great flourish and gush of conversation, helped his riders to mount.

They had a good ride. When they returned I told Joe to corral the horses and invited our friends to the front porch for a tall cool one. Our concrete work was finished, it was late afternoon and we'd all relish the relaxation and a good visit.

"Say, that's quite a boy you got there," said Dorine, as soon as we were comfortably seated. I shuddered and could see Lucy squirm a little.

"Yes, he *is* quite a boy. New man. Did he take good care of you?"

"Sure. We had a fine ride. But why hadn't you told us about your pack trips into the Superstitions?" asked Frank. I could hardly wait to hear more about our plans.

"Joe tells me that country is so rough you can't get through with horses and you're having some javelinas trained for riding and packing."

Oh brother. Here goes another whopper. Javelinas are wild hogs which roam in this country. A big one might stand thirty inches high and is meaner than a snake. Train one?

"Yes, the country is rough. What else did he tell you?"

"Said Jack Anderson had a whole herd of javelinas the size of burros down at the Apache Junction zoo and they are breaking and training them for you. Each hog would be broke to ride or pack, and they'd be good enough to travel in any of that country."

Frank seemed a little skeptical but he had arrived not long ago from New Jersey and if a guest ranch operator had undertaken this business of packing and riding javelinas, maybe it was possible.

"Joe said a saddlery in Mesa was making up special riding and pack saddles to fit the javelinas because ordinary saddles wouldn't do."

Lucy couldn't restrain herself from laughing, and when we told them of yesterday's fine speech and Joe's conversion to truth and light, they almost fell out of their chairs.

Early the next morning I went to Joe's camp and told him he was through.

"Why, boss? What did I do?"

"Just pack up and get the hell out of here."

They did. In mid-afternoon he returned alone in his father's jeep, picked up a pair of spurs he had left hanging on the front porch post, and off again without saying a thing. That evening I chanced to be in Apache Junction.

The bartender said, "Boy, I guess you're lucky to be alive."

"Why's that," I asked.

"That new man of yours came in this afternoon and had a half-dozen drinks, said he was going to up and beat the hell out of you for firing him. Said by God he'd bust you wide open so you wouldn't forget old Joe Dawton."

23

MURDER!

LUCY AND I PLANNED TO SPEND THE SUMMER OF 1947 building three new cottages. With the addition of modern conveniences such as electricity and indoor plumbing our enterprise was poised for expansion. We chose sites on high ground commanding a matchless view of the long valley stretching to the south. The cottages would be of stone and pine like our house, and each would sport a living room, dinette, bedroom, kitchen and bath with hot and cold running water, complete with a porch and sun terrace at each front door.

One of the men we hired to help us was a young Mexican boy named Angel Serna, but preferred to be called by his nickname, "Rocky." We bedded him down in the adobe house where Bates had lived. He made himself at home there and seemed to enjoy living alone. In the evenings he generally sat in his doorway and sang Mexican songs. We could hear him at the house, even though it was nearly half a mile away.

Lucy enjoyed working with the young fellows we had around the place and they enjoyed her company without ever getting fresh. She and Rocky soon were talking to each other in Spanish and he was having fun playing amusing little jokes on her. Almost daily he would do extra jobs to please Lucy, performing them after working hours without prompting, and without admitting he had done them. In fact when Lucy would try to thank him, he modestly denied knowing what she was talking about, but with a sly smile of admission on his face.

His infectious laugh disclosed a set of perfect teeth, shining like polished porcelain. He tried harder than most men to keep clean, and his clothes were as orderly as a working bachelor's could be.

By good fortune we had been able to obtain enough pipe to connect the well with the storage reservoir on the hill, and to pipe water to all the buildings as well as to the new cottages. This was a big job. Rocky said he had learned to plumb in the Army during the war, so I relied on his help. I also counted on him for the necessary pick and shovel work. Mexicans have been acclimated to the desert sun for generations, and Rocky soon proved that he could swing a pick into rocky ground for hours at a stretch on the hottest day without a pause in his songs. He had a varied collection; classics, love ballads and barroom ditties.

Rocky was a talkative fellow and as he worked told us much about himself. One of a large family raised in the Gila River Valley of southeastern Arizona, his parents were large landholders and there was a farm for him if he returned home, but that was not to his liking. He had preferred to roam after being released from the Army in 1946.

He was short, stocky and very strong. The muscles rippling under the bronze skin of his broad back were like steel. It was little wonder that he had found success in prize fighting, which he had given up at his Mother's request. As his story unfolded, he told of the many ways in which he had accepted her guidance.

As a boy on his father's farm he had learned to be a good horseman. I've never seen a better one. He helped take care of our horses now, and spent extra hours in early morning and evening around the corral. He and Paul worked together amiably, and the energy of each was a challenge to the other. The work fairly flew.

As we worked together through the summer months we came to think of him as a part of our family, and so great was our faith in him we never questioned giving him access to our house and all that we owned.

One day he handed me a letter to mail. Quite casually I noticed the address: "Board of Paroles and Pardons, Phoenix, Arizona." It struck me as a title to another story — a story I really didn't want to hear but must, for Lucy's safety and my own. I didn't know what to do. But for Rocky's complete confidence in me and forthright innocence (if the letter said what I supposed it did) the story might never have come to my attention. He was in town frequently and could have mailed dozens of such letters without our knowledge. He was either very naive or, I chose to believe, had successfully rectified any wrong he might have committed and had complete confidence in his future. I chose to not mention it to Lucy at that time, but I cautiously took her with me to drop her off to do some shopping when I went into Phoenix that day.

Instead of mailing the envelope, I delivered it in person. I told the Chairman of the Parole Board that Rocky was working for us under circumstances in which we either must trust him implicitly or let him go. I said that his work had been excellent, his conduct good, and that I had no reason to question his integrity were it not for this letter.

The man pulled out the file on Rocky's life and prison record. What the record showed concerning his early life and wartime activities coincided with what Rocky had told us. Then we came to the part which involved the Board.

He gave me a rundown of the information in the file. Serna and three other young Mexicans got drunk and robbed a small filling station at a desert crossroads in the southern part of the state. He and his companions were captured near the border. They put up no resistance. At the trial he made no effort to defend himself and would have plead guilty had not his counsel advised otherwise. He was convicted and sentenced to three years at the penitentiary in Florence.

When he was first eligible for parole, the Warden recommended that Serna be paroled based on his exemplary conduct in prison. He had never caused the slightest trouble and the Warden personally had observed him and his work. He felt that Serna had been sufficiently punished and could be trusted to be a good citizen on the outside. Accordingly he was released and put on probation until the following February.

"If he does anything he should not do prior to that time he will be sent back to the penitentiary. This letter is the monthly report of his whereabouts and employment," the officer said.

"Is there anything in his record indicating violence or any objectionable act when he has not been drinking?" I asked.

"Not a thing. When some people get one drink too many, they are easily influenced and I think he fell into bad company and followed them without personal malice or inherent desire to do wrong. It was a young man's spree that ended badly. In fact, I've seen cases in which white boys have done similar things without being taken so seriously," he said.

"I'd like you to put yourself in my place," I said. "We live a long way from anyone else in the desert. If I am not satisfied of our own safety I'll be rid of Rocky in a moment. On the other hand, if he has learned his lesson and is on the way to becoming a good citizen I would like to help him. To fire him based on his record might be an injustice, cause him to get back into bad company and perhaps land in prison again. What is your thought?"

"Of course there is some risk in anything of this sort, but in this case it seems to me even less than with another young man who has not had this experience. This boy is on parole and has to account for himself. He knows very well that if he doesn't behave, back to prison he goes. If you feel that you can do so, it would be in the Board's interest to have you keep him with you. He's away from trouble out there, and you seem interested in him."

I left with the feeling that we could help Rocky, that it was a good project which might bring us much satisfaction. We both liked the boy.

I told Lucy all about it and she agreed that we should keep him. We also agreed that we must be certain he did no drinking. The next morning we called Rocky onto the porch and I told him the complete story, including our reasons for letting him stay and everything the Board officer had told us. I also told him that if there were the slightest question about his behavior I would let him go at once.

I told him that I wanted his absolute promise that he would not drink on the ranch or anywhere else while in our employ. "You can't handle liquor, and will be in trouble if you ever try."

"Yes, sir, Mr. King, you can depend on me." He said it in full seriousness, and Lucy and I were pleased at his demeanor. As we shook hands to seal the bargain, I said, "We want to help you, Rocky, and we'll depend on your word. Don't break it."

We kept Rocky's past to ourselves, not even telling Paul. Several uneventful weeks passed, Rocky singing and working as always. Then one Monday morning he failed to return from his weekend in town. We hoped our fears weren't true, but our hearts sank. The only practical thing to do was to go to town and see what we could find out. I needed help and if Rocky had stepped off we'd have to get someone else.

I found him at the home of his relatives. He had been drinking over the weekend. The old man who was head of the family drank long and frequently; and was always out of work and money. He knew Rocky would have a pay check and collared him as soon as he came to town, inducing the boy to buy him alcohol.

It wasn't long before the old man lit Rocky's fire, which only now was dying slowly and painfully.

These were extenuating circumstances and we took him back after a firm warning.

A month later he was two days late returning to work. Investigation proved the old man had started trouble again, so we gave Rocky another chance following a firmer warning. But it was to no avail, and the night I discovered him drinking in the adobe house we had to let him go.

Rocky got a job at a gas station near Apache Junction. So far as we could see he was getting along all right. In the fall he started riding a filly named Linda in the quarter horse races at the Junction. He was a good jockey and she was fast. Rocky did not own Linda, but loved her and cared for her with skill and tenderness. Together they won race after race.

One night late in December I was detained in town after dinner and didn't get home until after ten o'clock. I greeted Lucy with, "Sorry I'm late. Some things in town I had to take care of. Anything happen today?"

"OH BROTHER, did anything happen?" A deep sigh escaped her lips. "Airplanes, squad cars, two women shot — DID ANYTHING HAPPEN!"

"Good Lord, what's been going on?"

"It's Rocky, Honey. He did something awful — just awful. It doesn't seem possible, but he did it and they've captured him. It's horrible."

Gradually the story unfolded. Rocky had come to the ranch about 4:30 in the afternoon on December 29, and showed up at Paul's bunkhouse near the corral.

"Hello, Paul," he had said. "I want you to take me to my mother's place in Safford."

"Why?" asked Paul.

"I've got to get there. I just shot two of them."

"Two what?"

"Two women. You got any ammunition?" He rolled the cylinder of a large revolver exposing two expended cartridges. Paul understood immediately. He looked at the car Rocky was driving and recognized it as one belonging to a woman who lived near Apache Junction. There was blood on Rocky's shirt sleeve.

"No, I don't have any shells that size." Four rounds of live ammunition were still in the gun.

"Get another car, Paul. They'll catch me in this one. I'll pay you to help me, but you've got to get another car."

"You drive back a mile to that little road that goes off to the west. Hide that car down there and stay in the brush where nobody can spot you. I'll get another car and pick you up. Stay out of sight." Rocky drove away from the bunkhouse.

Lucy said she saw Paul running up the road. When a cowboy runs uphill in cowboy boots, something is going on. Lucy met him on the porch.

"Get Julian's .30-.30 and .38. I'm going over and get Father King's car. Rocky was just here. He's shot two women. We've got to notify the sheriff. You take the .38 and come with me. I've got my .45 and I'll give the .30-.30 to Father King."

"For heaven's sake where is Rocky?" Lucy asked.

"He's hiding in the desert if he went where I told him to. I can lead the law to him if we can find the sheriff."

Lucy gathered the guns, gave Father the .30-.30, told him what was afoot, carried the .38 revolver herself and got into the car with Paul.

There was no sign of Rocky or the car anywhere in the three miles between the ranch and the highway. They turned west toward Apache Junction where they encountered a search party, including a deputy's car and the state highway patrol at Sand Tanks, a local gas station. Another party was working the desert with bloodhounds, and a deputy in a plane was searching by air. Paul told the officers what he knew and offered to lead them to Rocky's hideout. The officers insisted that Lucy stay at Sand Tanks.

Paul and the officers returned to the place where he had told Rocky to hide, but the car was not there nor were there tracks showing he had ever turned off onto the side road. Paul realized that Rocky may have doubled back. He knew where the horses were, and the cars, guns, and money. He might still be there. They all hurried toward the ranch, but halfway there spotted car tracks leading into the open desert. They followed the tracks and Paul spotted the car Rocky had been driving. The officers drew their weapons and surrounded the car, but it was empty. The circle widened into a search of the surrounding area but they had barely started when Rocky came walking out of the brush and surrendered with no resistance.

An officer told Paul that Rocky had shot and seriously wounded Mrs. Fairy Thompson during a holdup of her little store west of Apache Junction.

"Who's the other one? Rocky told me he shot two women," Paul told the officer.

"No, he only shot one — Mrs. Thompson."

Paul persisted, "That car he was drivin' looks to me like Mrs. Gohn's. He probably shot her, too." Rocky kept his eyes on the ground and said nothing.

Paul was determined. "There are two empty cases in his gun — take a look!"

The officer inspected the gun and found Paul was right, but it was late that evening before they went to Mrs. Gohn's and found her mutilated body in the midst of a scene of life-and-death struggle.

Soon the story was pieced together. Rocky's current employer said the boy was desperate to own Linda, the little horse he had been riding. The owner was going to sell her and he had tried to borrow the money from him to buy her. When he refused, Rocky took off, vowing he would find it somewhere.

Mrs. Thompson said he came into the gas station at noon and told her it was a holdup.

"Put that gun down and quite playing jokes, Rocky," Mrs. Thompson said as he pointed the gun at her. Rocky said nothing — just glared at her and pulled the trigger. Mrs. Thompson fell, the bullet passing perilously close to her heart. He ran out of the store and disappeared on foot into the desert toward Mrs. Thompson's mother's house, Mrs. Gohn, where he cold-bloodedly raped and murdered the widow and stole her car.

Paul was the chief witness for the state in a trial that was run through in a hurry. The jury found Rocky guilty of first degree murder, sentenced him to death by gas and placed him on death row at the penitentiary in Florence. Months passed during which the case was appealed to the Supreme Court, but the conviction was upheld.

Rocky sang his Mexican songs in his cell before and after the trial. He refused to tell his attorney anything which might exonerate him or aid in his defense. He acted strangely detached from everything going on around him, almost as though all of these things were happening to someone else.

It was not long before the detective magazine writers descended upon the ranch to interview and photograph Paul and me, and shortly their story was headlined on the front of pulp magazines under blazing captions: *Killer Beast of the Superstitions, Heinous Murderer Amuck in the Desert.* The headline writers had a field day.

At Christmas time there appeared among our greeting cards an envelope addressed to Julian and Lucy King. In the return address space appeared, "No. 613971, Florence, Arizona." The card inside bore an engraved Christmas message of tender good will. It was our last word from Rocky. We both wept just a little.

Rocky marched stoically to his execution with no explanation or word of repentance ever passing his lips. The state had built a new gas chamber at the prison, and if it were possible for any emotion to penetrate that protective armor of impassivity, Rocky probably enjoyed a certain wry satisfaction in being the first occupant of that grim cubicle.

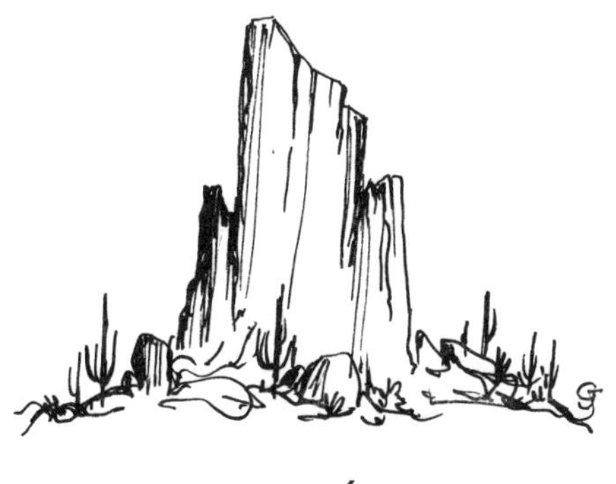

24

Horse Thievin'

I think Lucy's love for her horse "Cactus" originated in her instinct to protect a poor little orphaned animal who had the misfortune of starting his earthly tour with the name of "Lousecake." The name was an insult to any animal, and a particularly cutting jibe at such a nice little fellow as this colt was. She took his side in everything and it was not long before she chose Cactus whenever we went riding. He was all right, but had done nothing to attract Paul's or my attention until we decided to make an exploratory trip to the top of Superstition in quest of the ruin of a prehistoric Indian village.

Roy, a young photographer friend, had visited the ranch several times and said his interest in the Superstitions was first aroused when he was in an aerial photographic unit stationed at Luke Field west of Phoenix during World War II. He had photographed the Superstitions from the air in his many flights over the mountains. Now he wanted to take pictures from the ground, and we were making the trip together.

According to local accounts there was one canyon which might lead to the summit that might be reachable by horses. The reported location of the Indian ruins was some distance from the place where this trail topped out, but on the same ridge. We needed to work out the route for we knew dudes would like a horseback trip to the summit, the ruins, and across to famed Weaver's Needle, famous in local lore for being a key to the Spanish treasure and the Lost Dutchman Mine.

We decided to make it a four-day trip. Two pack horses were required to carry provisions, bedrolls and grain for the horses. Cactus had never been packed, but we decided to try him on this trip.

The lower half of Carney Canyon was not too difficult, but the higher we went the steeper the grade and the worse the trail. It deteriorated into a half-cleared shallow ditch eroded by rains, leaving loose, sliding rocks about the size of the crown of your hat. The footing grew so poor, the grade so abrupt, that we had to dismount and lead our horses.

Paul was riding an enormous sorrel which a friend had asked us to use. "The more work you get in him the better I'll like it. He's too much of a pet. I want to get all those silly ideas out of his head and get him toughened up."

The horse was a huge, powerful animal but he was not suited to the rocks and had no experience in them. He was in the lead, and in the sliding rocks found it almost impossible to gain a foothold.

Cactus was directly behind the big sorrel, carrying a rawhide pannier on each side of his pack saddle. He followed so well that we took off his halter and he was a free animal. His short, stocky legs were built for this kind of work, so he was having no real trouble in the rocks. I was on foot behind Cactus, where I could see every move he made. He amazed me with his ability to travel without strain on this rough trail, but I was never more surprised than when he moved up behind the big sorrel, put one of his pack boxes against the sorrel's rump, and pushed him through a difficult hundred-foot passage.

I called Paul's attention to it. Several times Cactus repeated the maneuver. The little guy had pure "horse sense."

When we eventually arrived at the summit we stopped for a needed rest. All the horses except Cactus were hot and tired, but he was still in good shape.

"Don't you tell Cactus' owner what he did," I told Paul. "I'm going to buy him and the price would double right now if he knew that horse pushed that big sorrel up the side of a mountain."

We bought Cactus at the first opportunity, and he was Lucy's horse from then on.

In late winter Cactus came down with distemper. We tied him away from the corral in an effort to prevent contagion to the rest of the herd, but all except one of the animals got sick and we had a horse hospital on our hands. I bought penicillin by the case load and all the horses except Cactus responded. He developed huge lumps just below his lower jaw bones and became deathly ill. Lucy made two or three trips a day to the corral to stroke his neck and talk to him and exercise him lightly. On one especially bad night, I had to dissuade her from taking a bedroll down to the corral to stay at his side. Paul and I both assured her that he would come and get her if she was needed.

As a last resort, the veterinarian injected a large bottleful of sulpha solution into Cactus. Normally the horse was a fighter, and I didn't think we would be able to hold him quiet for such a procedure, but the sickness and fever had stolen his spirit. Cactus stood like an "End of the Trail" statue as the doctor lanced the swellings in his neck. He seemed to recognize a helping hand.

The next day the colt showed some improvement and Lucy took him for a longer walk. Her spirits rose as Cactus gradually recovered. As soon as he was able, she led him to the house. The guests, some of whom had shown as much interest in his illness as they would have the President's, all came out and petted him and fussed over him. He responded like magic. When Lucy started leading him back to the corral he suddenly rose on his hind legs, nickered, and jerked the rope out of her hand. Off to the corral he went at full gallop, made several rapid circuits, kicked up his hind quarters and stopped by the hitching rack.

Lucy stood in the road watching him. Tears welled in her eyes and ran down her cheeks. There no longer was doubt of her pet's recovery.

I had a gift for being away from the ranch when big trouble was brewing. Errands had taken me to town and Lucy was visiting a neighbor when a slightly built young man approached Father's house from the north, an unusual occurrence because the road lay to the south. The July sun hung over the desert with a fiery vengeance, yet he was afoot and bare headed and as he came closer, Dad could see that he was apparently Chinese.

"Barney Barnard said I could rent a horse here," he told Father, "and ride to Hieroglyphic Canyon. I've read about the pictures on the rocks and would like to see them."

"We have horses for rent," Father said. "Julian is gone but I guess I can saddle a horse for you. I noticed you walked in from the north. Where did you come from?"

"I walked over from Barney's. I'm a guest at his ranch, staying there until my wife comes from New Orleans."

Barney Bernard is a good friend of ours. He often brought his guitar to the ranch and entertained us with his repertoire of western songs. Dad decided that if this boy was Barney's guest he should have the best, so he caught up Cactus and put Lucy's saddle on him.

The ride to Hieroglyphic Canyon is normally a two-hour ride.

"It's pretty hot. You better take a canteen of water with you." Dad took down one of the canteens, filled it with cool water and tied it to the fork of the saddle. Then he led the young man, whose name was Wung, to the beginning of the trail, gave him full directions and bid him good luck.

When Lucy returned at 5:30, Father told her about the incident. She allowed as how Chinese cowboys were a little scarce this season, but went about her normal activities.

6:00 came, 6:30, and finally dark, but Cactus and Wung did not show up. Lucy and Father grew uneasy and Mother felt certain something was wrong.

"There's something phony about that fellow," she told Father. "You've got to get Cactus and Lucy's saddle back for her somehow."

Of course there was little he could do, and I was still in town, happily oblivious of the tension at home.

Father got in the car and drove to Barney's to find out if this man was who he said he was.

Barney said he didn't know much about Wung, but he had stayed there a few days and was expecting his wife from New Orleans. That all matched with what we had been told. He said that Wung had been reading about the Lost Dutchman gold mine, the Spaniards, and Apaches. Barney rightly had told Wung we were the only folks in the vicinity with horses to rent, but we never let our horses go into the interior of the Superstitions unless our guide was along. The country was rough and it was too easy to get lost. He had told him that King didn't worry too much about the riders, but he sure didn't like to lose his horses or see them get hurt.

I returned home between 9:00 and 10:00 that night and found Mother, Father, and Lucy in a first class tizzy. Lucy tearfully was trying to comfort Mother, Mother was trying without success to comfort Lucy. Father was side-stepping desperately, but had been caught by more than one of Mother's sermons on the text, "You should have known better than to let that Chinaman have Lucy's horse." He, particularly, welcomed me home. By now everyone was trying to say the right thing to get out from under.

The night was black as a horse-thief's heart, and I could see no way to help the situation at that hour. I suspected that Wung had headed into the mountains where there would be no chance of finding him before dawn.

"I'll saddle Star at sunup and start tracking," I told the family. "I can't get far tracking by lantern light, so let's all go to bed and I'll find Cactus tomorrow."

I comforted Lucy as best I could, but about all she could say or think was, "Poor little guy, I hope that Chinaman feeds him and finds him water." There was nothing else to do, so we all turned in.

The monsoons hadn't come to the desert yet and there was reason to be concerned about water for Cactus, although he was a tough little horse and could stand as much as any. No one worried about Wung. He could take care of himself.

At sunup Star and I easily picked up Cactus' tracks and followed them at a trot along the Hieroglyphic Canyon trail. Presently I found where they had backtracked, then headed east. I followed about two miles. Their direction was constant and indicated that Wung was riding along the face of the Superstition's escarpments, looking for a way into the interior of the mountains. The trail had lost its freshness, evidence that Wung was well ahead of me. I was sure he would find Peralta Canyon and take the trail which the Spaniards had followed into the mountains a hundred years before, so returned to the ranch and picked up a car. I drove to the foot of Peralta Canyon as quickly as possible and found Cactus' hoof marks. They were old enough to convince me Wung had a long start ahead of any pursuers.

I drove back home for provisions and Lucy. Putting ourselves in Wung's place, we reasoned that the rugged Superstitions, the heat and thirst of the July day, would discourage him. Possibly he would lose his way. In that event Cactus would head for home. Wung's adventurous spirit would be gone, he would let the horse have his head. If he didn't, Cactus was the kind that would dump Wung in a cholla and take off for home on his own. The horse knew the mountains well and certainly would head for the foot of Peralta Canyon, where he would be stopped by a fence.

It was late afternoon as we approached the small desert ranch at the base of the canyon. Lucy's eager eyes spotted Cactus tied to a tree by the corral. Wung sat on a rock beside him. I could feel Lucy's elation from three feet away as she spied her colt.

I didn't know if Wung classified himself as a horse thief, but we approached him as such. One cannot track horses across a blazing desert in July and have much sympathy for a guy who is foolhardy with himself and cruel to a good horse. I was mad. Just plain, stinking mad. So was Lucy.

When we came close enough to see clearly in the gathering dusk, it was apparent that Cactus' hindquarters were badly cut and that he was in a grievous state. You could put both your fists in the hollow of his flank. Lucy saw red.

"Where have you been with my horse? How did you cut him? Why didn't you feed him? The poor little guy hasn't had water in a day and half, and look at you sitting there beside that canteen. You look just fine. You got feed and water, but how about my horse? You just let him suffer? Look at Cactus. Just look at that poor little guy. And you probably think you're a man!"

She lashed Wung with every scorching phrase she'd thought of during a sleepless night, but I could see the tears welling in her blue eyes as she realized Cactus' plight.

Wung was well supplied with food, blankets and cooking utensils — everything he needed.

"Look at you!" she continued. "Of all the no-goods I ever met, you beat all!"

I didn't feel too good about Wung's future at the moment, because she was holding my .38 in her right hand.

"Where'd you get that equipment you've got?" I demanded, as I searched him for weapons. I removed a knife with a six-inch blade.

"They belong to Barney," Wung admitted. I inspected his gear. In one of Barney's pillow slips were a dozen or more cans of food and inside his jacket was an iron skillet, coffee pot, and German bayonet in a scabbard. Wung admitted all these things belonged to our neighbor. Barney was not at home when he left, so he excused his possession of these items by saying that he couldn't ask his permission to borrow them.

It's mighty irritating to have your work interrupted by an adventuring young man who fools you into stealing your best horse and saddle. You kind of begin to look around for ways to get even. Wung wouldn't weigh more than a hundred pounds if you dunked him in molasses, so there wasn't any satisfaction in hitting him. He admitted every charge we made, so you couldn't knock his teeth down his throat for lying. There wasn't much gratification in simply taking him to jail, but that was the only logical thing to do.

Our first duty was toward Cactus, the loyal little guy who never complained, who tried always to do what he was told and now had been sorely abused.

"How'd you get his flanks and rump cut up like that?" Lucy demanded.

"I got lost," he said. "Had no idea where we were or where we were going. I tried to make him turn off the trail and go east, but he wouldn't do it. He took off with me and came back here. I tried to get east again along that fence (pointing) but he wouldn't go there either. First thing you know we were in a tight spot between the fence, rocks and cholla cactus, and I got him into the barbed wire. I sure feel bad about that, but he insisted on turning and there wasn't much room. When I tried again to turn him he put up an awful fight and got into the wire."

"That horse was saving your miserable life, and you got him all cut up," Lucy said. "What's the idea of a guy like you going into the mountains alone, anyway?"

"Well," his voice and demeanor now begged for sympathy, "I've had trouble with my woman and there's nothing left for me to live for. Nothing. I wanted to lose myself in the Superstitions."

"My horse didn't want to die! And you didn't have sense enough to turn him loose so he could take care of himself? Oh no! You'd have tied him to that tree where he couldn't get feed or water, and then you'd have died in peace. Some humans don't deserve to have a name!"

Her lower lip quivered and so did her right hand, which still held the .38.

"We have to take care of Cactus," she asked, turning to me.

"There's no feed here but there should be water in the corral. We'll drive over to the Quarter Circle U and borrow a bale of hay. He's in no shape to take home tonight, even if we got the trailer. His right hind shoe is gone and he's all done in. We'll have to feed him and leave him here in the corral. I'll bring him home in the trailer tomorrow."

After watering Cactus, I left him with Lucy and the .38, took Wung with me in protective custody, and we drove the three miles to the Quarter Circle U Ranch and borrowed hay. When we returned, Lucy was stroking Cactus, rubbing the caked sweat from his back.

Grant's conquest of Richmond was a casual affair compared to Cactus' attack on the hay we'd brought him. His eyes lighted a little and for the first time, he acted like himself. We probably exaggerated in thinking so, but he looked grateful. If only a horse could talk.

It was past sundown, so we broke out our grub, built a small fire and put on a pot of coffee. Lucy opened a package of sandwiches and offered one to Wung. I thought she might have poisoned it, but Wung seemed to suffer no ill effects. We ate our supper around the fire.

"Wung, what would you do with a horse thief if you were me?" I asked. He hadn't really thought of himself in that light. The accusation set him back on his haunches a little.

He thought a minute and said, "Mr. King, I'm willing to pay you the rent for your horse, pay you for your trouble. Then maybe you wouldn't consider me a horse thief, and just take me back to Barney's. I want to go back there."

"You have no money, so far as I noticed when I went through your pockets and found that knife." I said. "How would you pay for anything?"

"I've got an uncle in California who bails me out of scrapes now and then, and I can get in touch with him."

"Oh, so you get in scrapes now and then?"

"Yeah, I'm wanted over in California now. You'd find it out sooner or later, I guess."

"What did you do in California?"

"Robbed a little store. Don't think there would have been any trouble about it but the man who owned it happened to be Justice of the Peace and he got out a warrant."

No question now about whether we'd take him to jail or back to the comfort of Barney's.

"Good Lord! You're real clever about keeping out of trouble," I said. "In California you rob the Justice of the Peace and then you come over to Arizona where horse thievin' has been a hanging matter ever since the first white man came, and you steal my horse. And I'm a Deputy Sheriff. Son, you're going to jail."

I drew a little satisfaction from thinking about how hot that crowded jail would be tomorrow.

Lucy got in the back seat of the car and Wung got in front beside me. Lucy laid the nose of the .38 on his shoulder with the cold muzzle touching Wung's left ear. She wasn't going to let this pigeon fly. We drove off.

I felt like an elephant bringing a flea into the sheriff's office in Florence. Wung's five-foot frame was skinny as a bunkhouse soup bone. The deputy took his belongings, which amounted to eight cents and a handkerchief.

I turned in the knife I had taken from him and the gear he had carried on the saddle. It was late at night and the deputy directed us to return in the morning and file charges. They threw Wung into the nearest cell. Lucy and I drove the 30 miles home.

Before returning to Florence in the morning we brought Cactus home in the trailer, then went to Barney's and I told him what had happened. He had been missing things, and the additions we could make to his list brought his slow burn to a white heat. He joined me willingly for the return trip to Florence to prefer charges.

The County Attorney was out of town and you can't file charges without him, so we turned into the Sheriff's office to check on Barney's possessions. Barney viewed the jacket, German bayonet which he had brought from France at the end of the first war, the canned goods, pillow case, hat, and flannel shirt, all with reasonable calm. Then he saw his little iron skillet.

"Why, that dirty, stinkin' skunk! He stole my little iron skillet. That dirty, lousy varmint!"

And then he added some more. The skillet in question was a valued treasure, the smallest of a nest of iron cooking utensils received from a friend.

A few days later we returned to do what we thought was our legal duty. Still nobody home at the County Attorney's Office, so we left again, and decided the County Attorney could come and see us sometime.

Our Chinese friend had fallen from grace in mid-July. The summer drifted by lazily and relief from the heat arrived in late September. By mid-October visitors were arriving in the Valley of the Sun and our callers were on the increase; we had been so busy we almost forgot about Wung.

In late October the Sheriff came by to notify us. "King, you'll have to come to Florence at once and do something about that Chinaman."

"Is he still in jail?" I asked.

"Sure he's still in jail. Been there all summer. But now they've got a habeas corpus and if you don't file charges right away we'll have to turn him loose."

"Barney and I tried three times to file charges, but never could find the County Attorney. Left word where he could find us."

"Didn't know anything about that, but we've got to act fast now."

"Okay, I'll go over and get Barney. We'll be in Florence first thing in the morning. Tell the County Attorney to stay home."

At 9:00 in the morning Barney and I were in the Courthouse.

"This man already has been in jail three months so I'd suggest you file petty larceny charges," advised the County Attorney. "You understand, however, that you have a right to file any sort of charges you wish."

Barney and I decided to go along with the suggestion, so charges were drawn covering the theft of Barney's gun and iron skillet. Trial was set for the next morning. The Attorney asked Barney and me to appear as his witnesses and to bring my father.

Florence is one of Arizona's oldest settlements. Its growth began in the 1860s and for a time it seemed destined to be the Territorial Capitol, but the advent of railroads diverted attention and growth to other communities. Florence settled into the more or less sleepy existence of a frontier cattle and mining town.

The Pinal County Courthouse looks like a picture in a history book. Built of soft red brick, it is a high-ceilinged affair decorated, on the exterior, with white ornate trimming. The roof looks like it had been gathered from the four corners and tied in a knot in the center. The cupola is adorned with a huge clock face. Until you look at the clock for a while, you don't notice that the hands don't move. When they built the courthouse in 1891, there was not enough money for a clock, so they painted one on. So it is always almost time for lunch in Florence, Arizona.

The interior is scrubbed and polished like a museum. There is a certain graceful formality about the high doors, thick walls, and broad staircase leading to the second-floor courtroom.

We took our seats in the front row of the spectator's section. The tall windows on three sides of the room were open to admit the pleasant October breeze. The judge's bench and the panel in front of the jury box were ornately carved, vintage, gay '90s. Counsel tables and chairs were of equal age, well polished and carefully preserved.

A few men were in business attire, but most wore Levi's and western shirts. An assembly of Stetsons crowded the hat rack, many with sweat-streaked bands, their crowns and brims bearing the caked dust of many Arizona summers.

The bailiff gave the signal to stand as the judge entered the courtroom. He was in shirt sleeves and smoked a big cigar. As he slouched onto the massive bench he nodded greetings to the voters in the room, flicked the ashes of his cigar onto the floor a foot or so from the brass spittoon, and settled back to see what the boys had to say.

A jury was chosen in a matter of minutes, the spectators lit their smokes and settled down for an interesting morning. Barney and I were sent into the hall and Father was called as the first witness. Barney was second and I was third. Each of us told our part of the incident. The defendant had no witnesses, made no presentation. The lawyers orated their summations and sat down. It was almost noon when the case was ready for the jury.

The judge spoke to the foreman. "Do you wish to take the case now — it is noon — or recess for lunch and take the case this afternoon?"

"We'll take the case now," said the foreman.

It was election year. "If you recess now and consider the case this afternoon, the County will pay for your lunch," said the judge with a philanthropic smile.

There was a buzz in the jury box. Evidently one of the woman jurors had a family to feed at home. "We'll take it now, Your Honor, if you please."

In ten minutes the jury was back in the courtroom with a verdict.

"Not guilty!"

A horse thief not guilty in Arizona? What's this country coming to?

A little judicious inquiry developed that one member of the jury thought three months in jail during an Arizona summer punishment enough. The other eleven members preferred lunch to a long argument.

Barney turned to me and said, "Julian, I didn't mind it when they called you a liar, and I didn't care when they called me a liar, but when they called Father King a liar. That's too much!"

We turned and went to the Sheriff's office where Wung was standing in front of the Deputy's desk signing a receipt for the return of his eight cents.

Barney's face was flushed as he turned to Wung and said in a voice that could be heard throughout the Courthouse.

"Wung, you get on a bus and get the hell out of Arizona. Don't let me ever see that silly face of yours again, understand?"

"Understand," said Wung.

25

A Busted Leg and a Book

EARLY IN THE SPRING PAUL AND I UNDERTOOK what became our annual contract of packing into the Superstitions for the Dons Club.

The Dons club is an organization of young business and professional men in Phoenix. Their interest is in perpetuating the legends and traditions of the Superstition Mountains, the Spanish Dons who had ridden into the mountains in 1847 and 1848 and discovered gold, and the Old Dutchman whose lost mine had caused violence and attracted prospectors for more than 70 years.

Members of the Dons Club annually stage an all-day celebration at the foot of Peralta Canyon for the public. For those equal to the trip they conduct an overnight hike to the interior of the rugged range, or a day hike to the head of the Peralta Canyon.

Our job was to pack in provisions for the overnight party and water for the thousand or more folks who took the shorter hike. On this occasion there were 34 bedrolls, cooking equipment, food, axes, shovels, and 80 gallons of water. The trail was so difficult for the horses that only two pack animals could be tied together in one string, so we had to make two trips into the mountains, but figured we could pack the equipment out in one trip on closing day.

Early on Saturday morning Paul and I rode out of base camp, each leading two pack horses. It was tough going in the rough spots, but we delivered our packs to the overnight campsite by late morning and came to the worst spot in the homeward trail just before noon.

I was in the lead riding Nugget. The giant sorrel gelding then was three years old, a powerful and high-spirited youngster, still relatively inexperienced in the rocks.

What happened next was all my fault. A rider can help his horse through a tough place if he will, but I guess I was day-dreaming when the trail led through a narrow, slick, rock basin.

Nugget placed his right front foot too high on the sloping slick rock. The iron shoe slipped and he tried to catch himself by putting his left foot higher on the slope. In a fraction of a second all four feet went out from under him. Down he went with his full weight on my right leg, pinning me against a sharp edge of the rock bowl.

I managed to hold Nugget's head down to prevent him from scrambling on that narrow ledge. I wiggled my leg from under him as his weight slid to the bottom of the bowl. Some way or other I hobbled to a stone bench within reins' length of the horse's head. I quieted Nugget as much as I could as he managed to regain his feet. Fortunately he had fallen to the right. To the left was a sheer drop of a hundred feet at the foot of which was a mighty uncomfortable mass of cat's claw, cactus, brush, and jagged rocks.

I looked at my right boot. The toe pointed west when it should have pointed south. I reached into the boot top and could feel the rough ends of jagged bones.

"Dammit, Paul, my leg's busted," I said. When I tried again to stand, I knew I couldn't.

Paul had dismounted and managed to worm his way along the narrow ledge past my pack string. He took one look at my off side and said, "There ain't a helluvamuch we can do but get you back on Nugget and head for home."

He was right. He checked Nugget out and found him sound, then led the other horses to broader ground. He brought Nugget to my side and helped me squirm into the saddle. He handed me the lead rope of my pack horses, remounted and took the lead with his pack string.

The trail was steep and brushy, particularly, I thought, on the right side where the useless leg dangled beside an empty stirrup. Back brush, ironwood stumps, boulders, laurel boughs, all reached up to take a whack at my foot. Each time they connected, pain shot up my leg until I wondered if I could ride as far as base camp without passing out.

We reached our destination in an hour and a half. The Dons' Club members were busy preparing the barbecue for the following day.

"Hullo, Julian. How's everything?" greeted my old friend, Louis Messenger.

"Just fine, Louis," I said, "except my right leg doesn't work so good." I pointed at my dangling limb.

This unusual news brought fifteen or more strong young men on the run. They bore all sorts of things with which to meet the emergency; but the most effective was a bottle of Scotch, which was not rubbed on the injured member.

Fred Guirey sprang into action and not only designed, but fabricated, an excellent splint made of mesquite sticks, my boot and a pot rag torn into strips. The 35-mile trip to the hospital was a comfortable one in Mel Compton's station wagon. My worst thought was of missing the Phoenix rodeo next Friday.

A hospital attendant, clad in white from head to foot, rolled a glistening stainless steel, white-wall wheeled stretcher, clad in a snow white sheet, to the rear door of the station wagon.

I told him, "You better take off that pretty white sheet before I get it all dirty and tear it with my spur."

"Don't worry, brother, you'll pay for it anyway, so you may just as well use it."

I stretched out on the spotless white linen, someone showed up with a hypodermic needle, and I spent an interesting half hour in the hospital corridor waiting for a mother to bear her child in the emergency room. This gave me a chance to get acquainted with a couple of nurses and to explain to half a dozen or more passersby why I was lying on that stainless steel marvel in the hospital corridor, complete with spurs, Levi's and Stetson.

While awaiting the newborn babe's wee cry, I was also accosted by the first of what was to develop into a long series of defaming remarks.

"What happened? Did you fall off your horse?" Words custom built to skyrocket the blood pressure of anyone who considered himself a decent horseman!

Lucy arrived while they were setting the leg. She generally comes up with something bright or funny on the slightest provocation. But this time she didn't. I'll always think the prospect of running errands for an invalid husband for three whole months (the doctor gave her this news as she entered) doused her spirits as well as her wisecracks. In fact, I fancied she sounded a little disappointed that I wasn't hurting somewhere. I guess it would be a bit of a shock to dash in, prepared to sympathize and comfort an anguished husband, only to find him having more fun than he did at home.

The medicos set the leg and poured me in a cast which stretched from my big toe as high as a Minnesota snowdrift in January. It was nice to see the toe looking normal, and I got some entertainment from watching it wiggle around. From the conversation between doctors, nurses and my wife I gathered that the reason for leaving it exposed was that if it turned black they would know it was time to cut off the leg.

News of my predicament spread by grapevine and one friend hastened to the hospital to cheer me. He wasn't much of a hand with garden flowers, so he brought Four Roses in a bottle. We planned a pleasant occasion before dinner, and I asked a passing nurse to please advise the kitchen I would like a rare steak. With a fishy eye she said, "Suurre," and kept on the move. I had fishcake along with everyone else.

But they must have a beverage alarm system in that hospital. A very important looking nurse soon appeared and with a "Dear me! We're-not-going-to-have-any-fun-here" look in her eye, headed straight for the drawer in which our treasure was hidden. Without breaking out of a full gallop, said, "Mr. King, I understand you have something which is prohibited here." The Four Roses vanished as in a desert windstorm.

That gal later turned out to be a whiz with the hypodermic needle, but at that moment I put her down as a dismal failure in the public relations department.

The next thing was a bed pan.

"What's that?" I was stalling.

"Your bed pan."

In a deep voice and my most determined manner, "Look, Sis, I'm 45 years old and I've never parked on one of those things yet, and I'm not about to start now."

"What will you do, then?"

A frightful thought must have struck her.

"You can help me onto that chair over there, push me into the bathroom and leave me alone."

"Well, Doctor didn't say you could, but he didn't say you couldn't."

So we did.

I managed to talk my way out of the hospital the next day, but it wasn't to be for long. Four days later they hauled me back, said they would have to operate and fasten the bone fragments together with screws. Dinner arrived about an hour after my arrival, then the evening shift took over and the parade of nurses with hypodermics, syringes, sponges, and charts lasted far into the night.

At 7:45 a.m. on March 14 the stainless steel lounge with four white sidewalls arrived at my bedside under the guidance of two new nurses. They looked pretty good, and I was glad to have such intelligent looking young ladies on my payroll.

I'll never get over marveling at the stainless steel carriage all swathed in freshly starched sheets. A $10.00 outfit probably would have gotten me there, but this thing was complete with controlled road clearance, ball-bearing swiveled wheels, and overdrive. They forgot springs and upholstery, however, and it was as uncomfortable a thing as I have ever had the misfortune of laying on.

Into surgery we went, and my conveyance came to a stop alongside the operating table. I raised on one elbow and looked around. Yes, there were further substantial additions to my payroll — four men all done up in white, everyone else in a white mask over his mouth and nose and I wondered what I had that they wanted. Why didn't they give me a mask, just in case I wanted what they had?

I soon found out who my new employees were. There were Number One and Number Two orthopedic surgeons. They were over on expense account from Phoenix, seventeen miles away. My local doctor was there on straight time, as was a very distinguished looking gent who announced he was the anesthetist.

A nurse, Number Five on the expense sheet, said it would take a little while to make preparations. That sounded like a feather-bedding deal inasmuch as five of the day shift would have to sit around and smoke cigarettes while one person did the work. I was relieved when the anesthetist looked at the available bottles and said, "Then let's use Sodium…." The last part of the name I didn't get. While I was trying to recall it, he sucked some of this fluid out of a rubber-topped bottle into a syringe, rolled me to one side, and bared the battlefield. A sharp jab dug a new foxhole before I could even flinch.

I said, "What did you say that stuff was, Doc?"

He said, "Sodium...." and I was out cold before he could give me the last word.

I guess my entire staff worked hard on the project, but I'll never know whether they padded the payroll or not, for it was 7:00 that night before I came to.

Next morning I was recovered sufficiently to discover the snow-white cast in which I was to be encased for the next ten weeks.

I began to look around for conversation. On the other bed in my end of the room lay a red-headed man of about my age, his right leg also in a plaster cast. His name was Jenkins and he was nice enough to ask me all about my troubles before spreading his. I told him all about my trip into the romantic and forbidding vastness of the rugged Lost Dutchman Mine country of the Superstition Mountains, and of my misfortune on the trail where the Spanish Dons had tread with their bonanza of gold more than a century ago.

I laid it on. Having been granted the stage all morning I finally reciprocated by asking him how he broke his leg.

I've met guys with all sorts of yarns about fortunes and misfortunes, but Jenkins is the first I've know who had his leg broken by an ostrich. Honest, I'm not trying to talk down on my own misadventure, or to build up Jenkins, but that is exactly what happened to him. He was in the wild animal business in Hollywood and had been hired to bring three ostriches to the Maricopa County Fair in Mesa. Prior to the daily horse show two male ostriches were hitched to racing sulkies. It seems ostriches won't just take off and run a race unless they are chasing another ostrich, so a female was turned loose to run around the ring while the boys chased her. On this particular day the old girl wanted to be chased and chased, and kicked the daylights out of

Jenkins when he tried to stop her! She shattered both bones in his upper leg.

Directly opposite my bed was another young man with a leg in a cast. Three of a kind in one ward! His break was a painful one resulting from an auto mishap, and most of the time he was in such misery that conversation for him was difficult.

The old gentleman in the fourth bed upset the routine of the nurses every few hours. He was pathetically cheerful, but his physical misery was almost complete. As nearly as I could gather without direct questions, he had sustained a serious abdominal operation in the course of which his puckering strings (I'm sorry I don't know the medical term) had been incapacitated. Each morning and a couple of times later every day it seemed inevitable that the nurses would successfully finish the bathing and bed-changing routine and then "the call" would come upon Mr. X. We all realized that his condition would not permit a quick emergency yank of the bell cord, so any and all of us who sensed the situation would pull our bell cords violently as quickly as possible. I have no doubt that the gadget on the other end of the cord was a quivering mass of wreckage by the time Mr. X. recovered.

The nurses realized that if they weren't quick, another hour of cleaning and bed changing was their lot.

The speed and efficiency of the nurses varied, but the fleetest one, oddly, was the largest. She could round the curve from the adjoining room on two wheels, pull up at the bed with smoking brakes and sliding tires, in one motion reach for the pan with her right hand and raise both Mr. X and the covers with the left without even killing her engine. If she had seen the green light quick enough and had sufficient traction to make a flying start, sometimes her arrival would be timely. If traffic was heavy or a red light intervened, however, there was nothing to do but get the clean-up tools and go to work.

Poor Mr. X could do nothing more than offer a feeble sigh, "Gosh, nurse, I done it again."

Jenkins and I started to make book. The big nurse soon became odds on favorite, but there was a little one who should have been much better, judging by what we could see of her chassis. Her consistent failures showed lack of coordination and odds on her soon rose to eight to one. The nurses didn't all share our macabre sense of humor.

By making myself a general nuisance I was able to win my second discharge from the hospital on the fourth day.

My brief absence from the ranch had been a tragic period for Mother. She is the dearest person on this earth, and her capacity for sentimentality exceeds that of anyone I knew. Her son's long and agonizing horseback ride after the accident, his first broken leg, his first trip to the hospital, the operation, surely the sum total of his agony was more than he could bear, she was convinced. Truthfully, I'd been in very little pain after the horseback trip out of the canyon, and outside of a bad disposition and complete impatience at being laid up, my suffering was limited to intense hunger for two hours preceding each meal.

But Mother was sure that only by prodigious bravery, by absolute self-control, was I able to shield her from the knifing, burning pain which must be coursing through my leg, up my side, back around my shoulders and down the other side into the good leg. By frequently examining my exposed big toe which those horrible doctors had painted a latigo brown, she was able to satisfy herself that the injury really was growing no worse.

Within a week it was clear that, being a prodigious correspondent, she had shared her sympathy with all our relatives, Lucy's relatives (of whom there were dozens), and most of our many friends and acquaintances. All, apparently, had been invited to notify me of their grief, for the mails started to bring stacks of sympathy cards, letters and gifts all intended to lighten my burden. They were sweet, and everyone appreciates the true friendship and sincere sympathy represented by all these wonderful expressions; but they all had to be answered!

The family and all the guests made wonderful preparations for my homecoming. The guests had collaborated in a fund providing an elaborate backrest so I could sit up in bed comfortably and read. The refrigerator was full of steaks, cauliflower, Mexican salsa, and all the delicacies I enjoy so much. Father had brought his favorite Morris chair for the day that I might get out of bed and sit up. There were piles of books, magazines, vases of flowers, several games, everything one could think of to make me comfortable and contented. Against the wall stood a pair of crutches.

When the commotion of homecoming was over Father, Mother, Lucy and Paul gathered around for a family conference. I thought I better get things organized, for chaos must have developed in the absence of my guiding hand.

"Heck," said Lucy, "we've missed you, but things have been going along as smoothly as ever while you were in the hospital. We were wondering what you've been doing all this time, that you could look so busy."

I still wanted to get my oar in somewhere, so I said to Father, "I've decided to make you Vice President in charge of operations. That makes you chief executive officer of the garbage detail. Paul will be your assistant. Paul, you're Vice President in charge of Horses. That means you gotta clean the corral every morning, do the saddling and take care of the guests' riding."

Paul said, "I've been doing that for some time now. Do I get any more pay with that title?"

"Not a helluvamuch," I replied. "Mother's in charge of mending, sociability, and comforting anyone whose 97-year old mother has died. Lucy'll take over anyhow, so there's no use me telling her what to do, just because I've got a busted leg."

I lay my head back on the pillow in the satisfaction that everything now was under control and I could confine my attention to avoiding the bed pan I'd noticed lurking among the gifts, and scratching the only two inches of my fiercely itching leg that

I could reach under the cast, which felt like a stovepipe lined with cactus.

The next day I sat up in the Morris chair and the guests got a good look at the cast, and my big toe. Of course they and all the visitors wanted to autograph the cast and they covered it from toe to thigh with all sorts of funny and sentimental statements. Blackie always watched closely and one day as I dozed he lifted his hind leg and added his bright saying just above the ankle.

Everyone was most attentive at first but that soon wore off and before long I had to suggest to Lucy the little things that I would like to have. A glass of cold water, my pipe, my cigarettes, a book, my pencil, a clean handkerchief, a cup of coffee, or a comb. The first few days it was "Yes, dear," "Right with you, Sweetheart," "Sure, honey."

A little later it became, "Yeah," "Okay," "Wait just a minute, willya?"

Within a week I sort of caught the feeling that they all wished I'd do something useful and by then I wished I could. This sitting around was deadening.

One of our guests who had been particularly appreciative of my stories of early days on the ranch even flattered me by suggesting that I write a book.

"You've got nothing else to do," she said. Once the seed was planted everyone started watering it with encouragement and several with insistence. Particularly Lucy. She wanted me to be occupied. While I questioned their judgment, the idea was interesting, even though it threatened to end my life of leisure.

Finally it came to the point where my pleasant loafing on the front porch was interrupted by sidelong glances and remarks such as, "Haven't you started that book yet?"

I was getting uncomfortable and feeling a little like a drone in a busy beehive.

Quick and Daisy came to see me.

"King, you look fine, except for that broken leg. Put a little meat on your bones in the last couple of weeks, haven't ya?"

Quick wasn't the only one who thought so.

"Guess I have, Quick. You and Daisy pull up a couple of chairs, sit down and tell me all the news."

"Well, we've *got* news," Quick's little finger was nervously picking at his right ear. "Me and Daisy got married by the Justice of the Peace in Coolidge couple of months ago."

Now he was fidgeting with the tops of his socks.

"And you know what? Daisy's expecting, that's all they are to it!"

"Wonderful!" Lucy shouted from the doorway where she was just arriving with a tray of cold drinks. I felt a little more like exclaiming "Remarkable!" recalling that sorrowful discourse Ma had plied us with before she left for Oregon, but restrained myself.

"Baby'll be born in October if everything goes as it oughta."

Daisy added, "Quick and I are so happy. Especially over the little fella. We've got a special place for him and a nice yard around our house in town. We've got electricity, running water and an inside toilet."

She fairly beamed with happiness after the longest speech we had ever heard her make.

She continued, "And look at my hands. The arthritis is all gone. I can peel potatoes, do my own housework, the yard work, everything. My neck's all right too. Look, I can turn my head as much as I want and it don't hurt at all. Quick sure fixed me up good."

We agreed that he had indeed fixed her up, and all congratulated Quick and Daisy. They accepted our blessings like manna from Heaven.

"Well, King, it's gettin' a little late in the afternoon and me and Daisy is goin' to take a quick look at a quicksilver prospect I located just before we left the desert. Don't suppose I'll ever work it but I might sell it for $50,000 or more if the right feller comes along."

The old prospecting glow was in Quick's eyes.

"Sure wish you was on your feet and could come look it over with us. What in tarnation you goin' to do with yourself the next couple of months while that leg heals? I'd think you'd be rarin' to go."

"Well, Quick, it looks like if there's going to be any peace and quiet around here, I'm going to have to write a book."

Epilogue

Julian

Julian was never happier than when he was creating something new. When a door opened, he and Lucy stepped through, devil take the hindmost.

Kings Ranch Resort was up and running by the end of the 1949 winter season. Arizona summers, inhospitable to year 'round vacationers, caused Julian and Lucy to again look west: to Catalina Island. In May of 1949 they opened P.K. Wrigley's Catalina Guest Ranch at Two Harbors, California, enticing my uncle, retired Air Force Col. Duran (Spike) Summers and wife, Ruth, a cousin and close friend of Lucy's, to join them as hunting guide and co-hostess respectively for three seasons.

At about the same time, under the Homestead Act of 1862, with $18 and the means to occupy and work the land, Julian acquired the 160 acres adjacent to Pearly's original claim. There he developed Kings Ranch Estates, a subdivision of acreages designed to accommodate the guests who wanted to own a piece of paradise.

In four years Julian had parlayed a $500 purchase for 80 acres into a 320 acre landholding. He had exchanged the $500 travel trailer plus closing costs for the rest of Pearly's claim. With the modest homesteading fee (the Homestead Act was rescinded by

Congress in 1976) the total price for a half section of prime Arizona real estate came to less than $4 an acre.

Word of mouth and publicity continued to attract guests and prospective buyers to the foothills of the Superstitions. The $500 sale that rescued Julian from returning to a desk job was followed by future land sales, keeping the resort afloat. The late Bill and Myrtle Storms and Judge Robert Cotton, whose daughter Martha and husband Larry Watkins still live on the property, were among the first guests converted to landowners. Many Kings Ranch Estates lots went to ranch guests, and some buyers just showed up, looking for a winter getaway in paradise.

In July of 1950, Ambrose and Caroline Lansing bought the first 10 acres on the homesteaded land, building their adobe home in 1952. The original house, now owned by their son, Cornelius and his family, burned in 2005. In August of 1952, my uncle Duran Summers, exchanged ten acres next to the Lansing property in payment for the $1500 my uncle had loaned Julian toward developing Kings Ranch Estates. Harry and Ruth Wilson bought 2.5 acres adjacent to the Summerses. The Kings retained 11 acres north of the Lansings. Except for the King property, which has changed hands several times over the years, portions of the rest are still owned by heirs and relatives of the original owners, including my husband and me. George Johnston, whose late wife Kit was a niece of the Lansings, and his daughter Carol Gilliam, live on a portion that land. Some of the Lansing property has recently been subdivided. The old-timers of Kings Ranch are dwindling in number. Steve and Betty Baldwin, son of early Kings Ranch settler Murray Baldwin still live in that home. Many later residents from the 1960s and 1970s also still live on the ranch.

In 1958, the Kings sold the resort to a Colorado resort operator, and built an art studio and home on their property next to the Lansings and Summerses. The resort also changed hands several times, undergoing a name change to "The Shadows" for a while. Tim and Beth Hopkins bought the resort and renamed it to Kings Ranch over a decade ago. It prospered for several years as a popular Elder Hostel.

Julian started a successful military and scholastic jewelry manufacturing company after selling the resort. He was an early investor in Apacheland Studios, which recently burned and is now a housing development. He held many prestigious board and commission positions before dying at age 65 in 1972 from cancer.

Lucy

The Kings' hospitality was legendary. Julian's talent for storytelling and gracious entertainment teamed with Lucy's earthy good humor and her fabled ability to whip up a feast from provisions on hand, drew visitors and raves from all around. She oversaw the preparation of their famous chuck wagon dinners for Dons Trekkers, the New York Giants training camp, and the Mesa Jaycees. Winter visitor gatherings for state reunions became popular during the 1950s, some attracting nearly 1,000 hungry tourists from all over the US and Canada.

After Julian died, Lucy stayed in their third home, her "dream house," built on a hilltop over the ridge to the north of the resort which enjoyed a nearly 360 degree panoramic view of the Superstitions and valley. A rapid health decline prompted her to sell the home and move to Mesa Christian Care Center where she was a patient for two years. Upon recovery, she moved into the Mesa Christian Villa retirement center where she lived for nearly 25 years. In 1981 she started the King Fund, which in 1986 became the Mesa Christian Care Center Foundation, to help residents whose financial resources are depleted so they can remain in the residence.

Lucy was an accomplished artist whose paintings can be seen at the Superstition Mountain Historical Museum and adorn the walls of many homes. She created and sold water-colored greeting cards well into her 80s. She was a popular public speaker at Mesa historic society events. She remained active in PEO and her Methodist church choir until she was nearly 90 years old.

She died on March 2, 1999 at age 93, two days after suffering a stroke. She maintained her vibrant, cheerful personality and earthy sense of humor until the end.

The Kings played an important role in the future development in Kings Ranch and Gold Canyon. Their concepts of how a home should blend into the landscape, retaining native vegetation, and constructing roads that flowed with the land can still be seen in the more innovative subdivision which now cover the slopes of the Superstition foothills. Where only 30 homes stood as recently as 1978, more than 12,000 have risen from the land. A population of 300 in 1986 has exploded to more than 23,000 in 20 years. Some residents live in mansions, overlooking the tournament grade golf courses that spill over Dinosaur Mountain and flow at the edges of the Superstition Wilderness. Others enjoy more modest homes, but nearly all express the gentle design and muted colors commanded by the brooding Superstitions and embraced by the Kings.

It is impossible to imagine what Julian might think of the manner in which this area has grown. His old "go get'em," zeal might lend a nod of approval, but one can't help but think he'd hold some reservations. As Lucy used to ponder as we drove her around the area on her frequent visits to our home in the 1980s and 1990s, "Julian must be spinning in his grave at how close these houses are." They may both be twirling as development climbs to the very edge of Kings Ranch Resort.

Land that once sold for under $10.00 per acre regularly goes for $100,000 per acre and far beyond. The gold in the Superstitions may not, as legend has it, lurk in the shadow of Weaver's Needle. Perhaps it lies instead in the rolling foothills, discovered by thousands of seekers of a 21st Century Shangri La.

Lucy asked me, during our last Christmas gathering at our home in 1998, to please turn Julian's manuscript, which she had given me many years earlier, into a book.

I offer you *"Sand in Our Shoes"* with the desire that it does justice to Julian and Lucy's hopes and dreams.

— Rosemary Summers Shearer, September, 2006